Anjum P. Saleemi argues that the acquisition of language as a cognitive system can only properly be understood by pairing the formal approach to learning, often known as learnability theory, with Chomsky's theory of Universal Grammar and its claim that human language is innately constrained, with some predefined space for variation. Focusing on specific areas of syntax, such as binding theory and the null-subject parameter, Dr Saleemi unites learnability theory's methodology with Chomsky's principles-and-parameters model, and construes acquisition as a function of the interaction of linguistic principles with largely domain-specific learning procedures, mediated by environmental input. Wexler and Manzini's set-theoretical approach is taken as a first approximation of a learnability theory of parameter setting. Acquisition is then hypothesized to consist of positive identification and exact identification, such that exact identification embodies the situation in which the correct grammar cannot be induced without an appeal to a richer learning system which involves some use of implicit negative evidence. The aim of this study is to show that a self-contained linguistic theory cannot by itself be psychologically plausible, but depends on a compatible theory of learning which embraces developmental as well as formal issues.

CAMBRIDGE STUDIES IN LINGUISTICS

Universal Grammar and language learnability

In this series

Supplementary volumes

Earlier issues not listed are also available.

*Issued in hardback and paperback.

UNIVERSAL GRAMMAR AND LANGUAGE LEARNABILITY

ANJUM P. SALEEMI

Allama Iqbal Open University, Pakistan

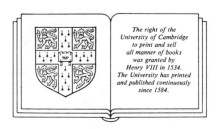

The right of the
University of Cambridge
to print and sell
all manner of books
was granted by
Henry VIII in 1534.
The University has printed
and published continuously
since 1584.

CAMBRIDGE UNIVERSITY PRESS

CAMBRIDGE

NEW YORK   PORT CHESTER

MELBOURNE   SYDNEY

Published by the Press Syndicate of the University of Cambridge
The Pitt Building, Trumpington Street, Cambridge CB2 1RP
40 West 20th Street, New York, NY 10011-4211, USA
10 Stamford Road, Oakleigh, Victoria 3166, Australia

First published 1992

Printed in Great Britain at the University Press, Cambridge

A catalogue record for this book is available from the British Library

Library of Congress cataloguing in publication data
Saleemi, Anjum P.
Universal grammar and language learnability / Anjum P. Saleemi.
    p.   cm. – (Cambridge studies in linguistics : 61)
Based on the author's thesis (Ph. D.) – University of Essex.
Includes bibliographical references and index.
ISBN 0–521–40075–9
1. Language acquisition.   2. Learning ability.   3. Generative
grammar.   I. Title.   II. Series.
P118.S175   1992
401.'.93 – dc20   91–4228   CIP

ISBN 0 521 40075 9 hardback

Contents

Preface

This book has evolved from my University of Essex doctoral dissertation. Much of the material has been reorganized, and a number of changes have been introduced, involving the omission of a good deal of background information and the addition of some new material. I have tried, at the same time, to preserve the essential character of the arguments as they originally appeared. I would like to thank a number of people for their help at various stages of (re)writing. Martin Atkinson, Vivian Cook, Michael Jones, and Mark Newson made significant contributions to the development of the dissertation on which this book is based. A special mention must be made of Gillian Brown, Iggy Roca and Keith Brown, who also provided invaluable support during the period of work at Essex. In fact, the help of all these people, in one form or another, has continued to reach me ever since. Furthermore, two anonymous reviewers for the publisher provided very insightful comments, as also did Teun Hoekstra, inducing me to reconsider most of the original arguments and to reformulate quite a few of them. I have also benefited from the information, inspiration and encouragement received from David Lightfoot, Ken Safir, Neil Smith, and Ken Wexler. Needless to say, I take full responsibility for the errors and omissions that may still remain.

The research that eventually led to this volume was carried out while I held a British Council fellowship, and was consequently able to be on leave from my job at the Allama Iqbal Open University. I appreciate the concurrent support afforded by both these institutions, without which I would not have had the opportunity to work on the ideas presented here.

Finally, I am indebted to the staff at Cambridge University Press for their understanding and professionalism, to Joan Baart for assistance in the correction of the proofs, and to my wife Nighat for help with the index.

1 *The problem of language learnability*

This book is concerned with the learning of language as a cognitive system, assuming Chomskyan nativism and employing conceptual and method-ological tools provided by the theory of learnability. Specifically, it seeks to explain the rationale, and present a demonstration, of the logical approach to the study of language acquisition in a universalist framework, with a considerable part of it focusing on the parameter-setting model. As we attempt to contribute to the ongoing debate on the learnability of natural language syntax, we indulge in a certain amount of syntactic analysis as well, but with the primary aim of optimizing learnability solutions rather than syntactic ones. Thus, weaving syntactic analyses into the formal fabric of the theory of learnability, this study is intended to show that a self-contained linguistic theory cannot by itself be psychologically plausible, and that such a theory will need to depend on a compatible theory of learning,[1] dealing with developmental as well as formal issues, if it has to have any cognitive pretensions at all. It seems that the best way to practise cognitive science, to which both linguistics and learning theories may be considered to belong, is to connect mental representations with related learning principles, analytical with procedural issues.[2]

We start off with a discussion of the basic puzzles of language learning, and in the process undertake an analytical review of certain key aspects of the linguistic and learning theories, thus paving the way for much that is to follow. Then we proceed to an in-depth analysis of the parameter-fixation model of language acquisition, firmly putting it in the context of a variety of learnability issues. In particular, we make an attempt to conceptualize parameter fixation (or parameter setting) as an explicit model of domain-specific learning.

The major current approaches to parameter fixation are critically examined, in particular the set-theoretical approach developed in Wexler and Manzini (1987) and Manzini and Wexler (1987), and the develop-mental approach of Hyams (1986). It is demonstrated that the approaches

1

in question suffer from certain serious drawbacks. The substantive view of parameter setting based on Wexler and Manzini's[3] subset principle and its auxiliary assumptions proposes a five-valued parameter in order to explain the cross-linguistic binding properties of anaphors and pronominals; it is couched in formal terms, is consistent with the standard 'no negative evidence' assumption, and views language learning as monotonic and deterministically conservative. We contend that the subset principle is much too rigid to be viable as a general-purpose mechanism of parameter fixation, and that the linguistic and learnability aspects of the null-subject parameter, the focus of a substantial part of the present study, do not appear to mesh readily with the Wexler and Manzini approach. Further, it is shown that Hyams's developmental view of the fixing of the parameter in question is untenable under a learnability approach, and that more convincing alternatives to her developmental analysis are available.

The null subject phenomenon is reanalysed from a joint linguistic and learnability point of view. Linguistically, the key aspect of the analysis is a separation of the identification and licensing of null subjects, with the optionality of Case and the resulting consequences for visibility in PF playing a central role in the process of licensing. The end-product of the linguistic analysis is a four-valued parameter, which can directly account for a wider range of linguistic variation than is possible under a binary-valued analysis. It is claimed that this multi-valued formulation has several other advantages over the traditional binary-valued ones.

Assuming this linguistic reanalysis, and taking the set-theoretical framework as a first approximation of a theory of parameter fixation, an alternative, and we hope more plausible, view of the setting of the null-subject parameter is developed. The alternative learnability framework involves a translation of some essentially formal aspects of the subset principle into more empirical terms. The crucial result is a markedness condition which is meant to replace Wexler and Manzini's subset condition. (This markedness condition is also shown to be applicable to the binding parameters as formulated by these two authors.) In contrast with the language-based view of Wexler and Manzini, the alternative involves a method of search of parameter values that is driven by the inspection of grammars, rather than languages, associated with the values. Furthermore, we argue that natural-language learning may involve inferential strategies over and above those embodied in simple parameter fixation. In particular, it is suggested that the auxiliary use of implicit negative evidence, i.e. negative inference from nonoccurring data, might be one of the legitimate learning strategies in a parametric model of learnability. The resulting augmented version of the learning model calls for a modification of the standard view of the child as an overly conservative language learner.

1.1 The theory of learnability

Language acquisition consists of optimal generalization from the available evidence, so that the conclusions reached by the child learner are neither too broad nor too narrow but just accurate. Torn between a persistent urge to generalize and an inherent call for restraint, the child might be viewed as faltering down the path of acquisition, simultaneously struggling with what he or she wants to do, what ought to be done, and what he can get away with for the time being. What kind of predisposition and learning strategies does the human child bring to bear upon this rather sensitive process, and how is it completed successfully and fast enough in the attendant natural conditions? Does the child operate on a lot of experiential stimuli and then gradually begin to formulate more and more domain-specific hypotheses, or is his or her predisposition to learn language so elaborately designed that only a minimum amount of evidence is sufficient to trigger the selection of the correct linguistic structures? Further, in terms of the logic of learning, how maximally complex does the minimal evidence need to be? Are one-clause sentences complex enough, or are sentences containing one (or more) embedded clauses necessary for complete and accurate learning? It is interesting to note that all these sub-issues emerge from a fundamental problem: how are human languages at all learnable under natural circumstances?

This problem is best studied in the context of an approach to language acquisition, embodied in what is known as learnability theory, that is basically concerned with *explaining the fact*, rather than *describing the course*, of acquisition (Pinker 1979). Evidently, this is very unlike the typical approaches to acquisition, such as most of those surveyed in Ingram (1989). Within a learnability framework the objective is to develop a 'principle theory', i.e. one that systematically analyses the general empirical conditions in terms of explicit theoretical principles, in contrast with a 'constructive theory', typical of the traditional perspectives, which is synthesized from relatively simple hypotheses essentially derived from direct observation of relevant data (Wexler 1982).

The somewhat narrower and considerably idealized mode of inquiry characteristic of learnability theory (e.g. Wexler and Culicover 1980), however, does not indicate an intention to exclude consideration of the actual processes involved. Generally abstracting away as it does from the development and maturation of linguistic and collateral nonlinguistic factors, in fact its ultimate aim always is to fit into some explanation of the developmental course of acquisition. In Morgan's words, 'learnability is but one condition that a successful theory of language acquisition must satisfy. In addition such a theory must provide an accurate developmental account' (1986: 169). But, given the forbidding complexity of the process of language learning, the task of explaining learnability would appear to be logically prior to that of explaining learning or acquisition in real time, since, as Pinker (1979) points out, 'it may be necessary to find out how language learning *could* work in order for the developmental data to tell us how it *does* work' (ibid.: 280). Pinker explains that

a theory that is powerful enough to account for the *fact* of language acquisition may be a more promising first approximation of an ultimately viable theory than one that is able to describe the *course* of language acquisition, which has been the traditional focus of developmental psycholinguistics. (1979: 220)

The major issue that learnability theory tries to resolve is the problem of learnability of natural language, what has been variously called the logical problem of language acquisition (Baker and McCarthy 1981, Hornstein and Lightfoot 1981b), the projection problem (Baker 1979, Peters 1972), and more recently Plato's problem (Chomsky 1986a, 1988) – indeed what may appropriately be renamed *Chomsky's problem*. The problem may be stated as follows: how can we explain the fact that every human child acquires the ability to comprehend and utter an infinite range of the sentences of any arbitrary natural language he or she is exposed to, although the data available to him cannot fully determine the state of the knowledge attained? First language acquisition is a curiously robust phenomenon. It occurs universally, under extremely diverse linguistic, psychological and social circumstances, and almost always successfully, despite the fact that the data provided to the learner are poor and degenerate. The external conditions of first language acquisition do not appear to be able to account for the deterministic success of the process, which typically is somewhat out of step with the input data and appears to have an internal dynamic of its own (cf. Newport, Gleitman and Gleitman 1977).

A standard position in learnability theory is that it would be pointless to try to conduct research on the learning of syntax without getting involved to a considerable extent in the fundamental questions of syntactic theory. Wexler and Culicover state that 'without a precise characterization of what is to be learned, the question of whether it can be learned is virtually meaningless' (1980: 486), in part echoing the following remarks by Chomsky that appeared in his famous review of Skinner's *Verbal Behavior* (1957).

It is futile to inquire into the causation of verbal behavior until much more is known about the specific character of this behavior; and there is little point in speculating about the process of acquisition without much better understanding of what is acquired. (Chomsky 1959: 55)

Although a good deal of first language acquisition research suffers from a lack of theoretical rigour, a small number of researchers (e.g. Morgan 1986, Pinker 1982, Wexler and Culicover 1980) have not shied away from confronting the problem of language acquisition in a principled fashion; also, some attempts have been made, notably Pinker (1984), Borer and Wexler (1987, 1988), to integrate language learnability and language development. In short, we believe that, even to be able to begin to ask the right kind of questions, it is necessary to take into account substantial assumptions regarding the form and structure of language.

An important result achieved by learnability theory is that it is hopelessly difficult to demonstrate the learnability of natural-language syntax merely on the basis of unbiased induction on observed evidence (Wexler and Culicover 1980). As Chomsky and Miller pointed out years ago,

To imagine that an adequate grammar could be selected from the infinitude of conceivable alternatives by some process of pure induction on an infinite corpus of utterances is to misjudge completely the magnitude of the problem. (1963: 277)

Humans often ultimately learn much more than they are exposed to, told, or even taught. The highly abstract knowledge of language achieved is underdetermined by the relatively poor experiential stimuli, which are deficient in many fundamental respects; for instance, in containing incomplete utterances, in being finite, and in *not* containing any overt evidence for the structural relations involved in rare or ambiguous constructions, paraphrases, and the like (Hornstein and Lightfoot 1981a). Further, it is commonly believed that only positive evidence, and virtually no negative corrective feedback, is available to the learner (e.g. Baker 1979, Brown and Hanlon 1970, McNeill 1966, Pinker 1989, Wexler and Culicover 1980).

Where does this knowledge in excess of that exhibited by experience come from? One plausible answer is that the basis for such knowledge exists prior to any learning, i.e. innately, and therefore the induction of grammar is nontrivially preempted by a highly restricted search space.

The thesis of the preexistence of domain-specific structures is attractive for several reasons, the foremost of course being that it appears to be correct. Secondly, heuristically it is the best working hypothesis; a domain-specific theory can always be modified, generalized, or even abandoned, if further evidence increasingly appears to support a more general theory, but the converse may not be possible. Morgan points out that 'we have much more to lose by wrongly adopting the general view than we do by wrongly adopting the specific view' (1986: 17). Finally, in our current state of knowledge a domain-specific theory is more feasible; it would be unwise to ignore an explicit specific theory in favour of a general theory that does not yet exist, and indeed may never exist (see the contributions to Piattelli-Palmarini 1980 and Demopoulos and Marras 1986 on these and related issues).

1.2   The interaction between linguistic and learning systems

The development of cognitive systems is of interest for several reasons; the most significant among these, to my mind, is that it may shed light on the structure of human cognition. One way this might happen is if it comes to be established, as a result of the study of its development, that a cognitive system is virtually unlearnable unless a certain amount of a very specific predisposition to develop it is assumed to exist prior to any exposure to environmental experience. This indeed is the claim that has been made, and to a reasonable extent substantiated, within the universalist–generativist paradigm of language acquisition. To indulge in oversimplification, suppose that X, a property of some natural language(s), appears to be learnable, and Y, another linguistic property, can be conclusively shown to be *un*learnable. Then one would be justified in hypothesizing that X is learned in some manner from evidence, and that actually Y does not have to be learned at all, being in point of fact a component of the learner's innate predisposition. Similar heuristic methodology, applied reiteratively to all the linguistic properties, should yield an inventory of the properties that may, in large measure, be environmentally induced, and another one of those that do not require such induction, thereby leading to a specific view of the pre-stored, i.e. pre-experience, competence of the learner. The puzzle to crack, then, is: how much of a cognitive system is innately determined, and how much open to experiential stimulation?

A *reductio ad absurdum* of the innatist view may run like this: everything that is learned, or is potentially learnable, must be innate. Taking language acquisition as an example, one could say that all languages (German, Kannada, Navaho, etc.) are innate as such; they are only 'rediscovered' from corresponding experience. Such a position, though logically possible, would be clearly untenable on grounds of both common sense and empirical fact.

A less extreme, and more realistic, view is to postulate the greatest possible degree of predetermination, necessitating that we devise a representational model that maximally accounts for cross-linguistic facts, with procedures playing a minimal role. This is exactly what the standard practice is among the linguists of the universalist–generativist persuasion, and the one I endorse myself in general. Such linguists study linguistic data with a view to uncovering the underlying principles and rule schemas; they also try to take into consideration, though perhaps not as often as one would like, the role of (positive) evidence available to the learner, in particular that subset of it which might have a triggering function.

Clearly, to assume the nativist hypothesis requires that the learning of the variation among natural languages should somehow be accounted for, as the child learner must be equipped with mechanisms that eventually lead him or her to the knowledge of one from a variety of possible languages. This issue may be resolved either by constraining the linguistic theory too narrowly, or by shifting some of the explanatory burden to the system of selection and evaluation of grammars (Grimshaw 1987). We maintain that less attention has been paid to the latter than appears to be theoretically warranted, and that no linguistic framework, however restrictive, can ever entirely dispense with some sort of learning theory, though the best part of such a theory, one strongly suspects, is likely to be domain-specific. More importantly, what is paid attention to considerably less often is the set of computational procedures that must be there – even for the purpose of the most rapid triggering to come about – to enable the learner to detect, operate on, and react to the relevant evidence in an appropriate manner. That general-maximal learning, for instance in the behaviourist sense, was a bad idea is no reason to conclude that specific-minimal learning is uninteresting or unimportant. What is minimal in comparison with a maximal view may nevertheless be substantial enough to bear on our theories of language on the one hand, and of language acquisition on the other. Furthermore, contrary to the usual assumptions, it is hardly self-evident that triggering is always a simple process. No doubt infinitely less problematic than totally unfettered learning from largely external sources, it may nevertheless be less of a smooth process than is generally thought, involving inductive problems of notable complexity and requiring decisions on the part of the learner that are quite intricate.

Postulating explicit learning procedures can, in short, provide us with a choice between: (a) an exhaustive but complex theory of language dependent upon a negligible learning component and a highly restrictive view of experience involving positive-only evidence; and (b) a simple but less comprehensive linguistic theory that requires an augmented learning theory with a somewhat less conservative view of evidence. The question as to which view to prefer is not an easy one; it of course raises empirical issues which cannot be resolved by stipulation. Even so, it does provide an option, where none will otherwise be available. A major goal of this book is to explore options such as this one, and to show how significantly the trade-off between the theory of language and the theory of acquisition can impinge on our conception of the cognitive system in question.

As the relationship between learning and specific knowledge structures is far from widely understood, we shall now explore different learning models varying with respect to specificity, taking a basic, general model as our starting point.

Learning is the process whereby a learner converts appropriate evidence into the knowledge of something. The evidence constitutes the input to the learner, and the knowledge the output of the process, as shown in (1).

(1) DATA   → | LEARNER | →   KNOWLEDGE
     Input   Output

The evidential data consist of a finite set of particular examples relating to the object of learning, such as a natural language. In the nontrivial cases, from this particular, finite evidence the learner is able to induce a general, highly abstract framework of knowledge with infinite performance potential, an example of which is the grammar of a language. Such knowledge is much broader in scope than the data that apparently serve as the inductive base. Learning is thus the process of *identification* of whole knowledge structures from partial information.

Compared to the nature of the knowledge system learned, it is relatively easy to study the properties of the input, though it is not easy to establish which ones of these are absolutely necessary for the process to occur successfully, and which merely facilitative (Morgan 1986). The reason for the indeterminacy is that it is very difficult to establish direct correspondences between the evidence presented to, and the knowledge acquired by, the learner. In the more interesting cases of learning, such as language learning, the chasm between the input and the output of the learning process is often enormous, exemplifying what earlier on was referred to as Chomsky's problem.

1.2.1   The empiricist paradigm

The behaviourist–empiricist answer to the problem was that the human learning system, i.e. the mind, is almost a *tabula rasa* prior to learning, and that it learns whatever it learns *ex nihilo*, by forming associations, analogies, and the like, provided sufficient reinforcement is available (see e.g. Skinner 1957). In other words, it was assumed that the learner's initial state was highly impoverished, comprising nonspecific learning strategies of the kind mentioned above. This evidently meant that learning was largely data-driven and that a learning theory LT for a cognitive domain D_1 was the same as the one for another domain D_2, or D_3, and so on. The highly general learning strategies attributed to the learner were of course considered inherent, but other than these no domain-specific innate knowledge was assumed. The empiricist view is schematized in (2).

(2) DATA   → $\boxed{\text{LT}}$ →   KNOWLEDGE OF ALL DOMAINS

Note that since no *a priori* assumptions are made about the learner's inherent predisposition to learn something, this model in principle allows a totally unstructured hypothesis space, thereby making the task of learning in any domain immensely difficult. No matter how large the battery of heuristic procedures, it seems unlikely that uninformed induction can result in convergence on an object of learning rapidly and accurately, especially so in the highly complex domain of language (Chomsky 1959; see also Catania and Harnad 1988 for a recent reappraisal of Skinnerian behaviourism).

1.2.2   The rationalist approach

As has been convincingly argued by Chomsky (1976, 1980, 1986a, 1988), Fodor (1975, 1983), Pinker (1982, 1984) and Wexler and Culicover (1980), among others (see Felix 1987 for a review), it is extremely difficult to demonstrate the learnability of any complex cognitive system like language merely from environmental input. If the linguistic knowledge attained is not a function of the environment in any significant sense, then a substantive amount of predetermination is highly probable, at least in principle.

One alternative solution to the learnability problem would be to posit learning mechanisms more powerful than associations, analogies, etc. But as has been pointed out (e.g. by Wexler and Culicover 1980), delineating more powerful mechanisms may not really be a way out; it is likely to contribute to the enrichment of the learning system to such an extent that the system will merely become an alternative way of attributing to the learner a highly articulate and predetermined initial state. One might as well, therefore, modify the conception of the language learning process by incorporating in it (as we do below under (3)) a component representing relevant *a priori* knowledge, clearly Universal Grammar (UG) in the case of language, which would considerably reduce the task of learning from brute-force induction over an unlimited hypothesis space to guided and informed learning, operating with a highly structured and restricted search space and a limited heuristic.

(3) DATA   → | LT   +   UG | →   KNOWLEDGE OF LANGUAGE

Arguing for limiting the hypothesis space over strong, or even intelligent, heuristic procedures, Chomsky and Miller write that

> The proper division of labour between heuristic methods and specification of forms remains to be decided, of course, but too much faith should not be put in the powers of induction, even when aided by intelligent heuristics, to discover the right grammar. After all, stupid people learn to talk, but even the brightest apes do not. (1963: 277)

Chomsky (1980, 1986a, etc.) goes so far as to make the bold claim that language learning is not a subcase of learning at all; the language faculty is a mental organ which instead grows, like a physical organ of the body, with the environment providing only the triggering stimuli. According to

Chomsky, a 'learning' model for language need not have a learning component at all, as illustrated in (4), where θ indicates the absence of a component.

(4) DATA → | θ + UG | → KNOWLEDGE OF LANGUAGE

On his view language learning is not caused by *any* learning mechanisms in any significant way; UG is (vacuously) its own learning theory in the sense that the problem of language learning was preempted phylogenetically and substantially taken care of in the course of biological evolution. Therefore the human child is spared the impossible effort of trying to recreate language from scratch in a relatively short span of his or her early life (Lightfoot 1982, Piattelli-Palmarini 1986, 1989). UG is hypothesized to consist of a finite set of principles and parameters. The principles lay down the fundamental features of natural language, whereas the parameters embody their variability, in that they offer a limited range of choices as a consequence of which languages may differ by taking one of the permitted values of each parameter.[4] Presumably this considerably reduces the problem of induction of language and empirically circumscribes the linguistic knowledge that can be naturally attained (Chomsky 1981, 1986a, 1988, etc.). Given such inherent principles, the class of human languages may be highly constrained; at least the number of possible (core) grammars of natural language could conceivably be finite, probably fairly small (Chomsky 1981: 11; cf. Osherson et al. 1984, Pinker 1982; but see Pullum 1983 for a contrary view, also cf. Wexler 1981: 46–7).[5] Clearly *a priori* limitation of the variety of grammatical systems is significant insofar as it might narrowly restrict the child's search for the correct grammar.

1.2.3 An augmented view of nativism

Although in essence we agree with the rationalist view, we suggest that, taken as a computationally explicit hypothesis about language learning, it is perhaps less than complete. It is indeed very likely that specific preexisting knowledge is an essential prerequisite for any plausible theory of language acquisition, but it is not quite clear whether the thesis of absolute genetic predetermination is able to truly capture the natural complexity of the problem. Specifically, if we assume that the language faculty is potentially capable of yielding variable knowledge but that

$LT = \theta$, then it follows that there is no learning mechanism for converging on particular languages (i.e. English, French, Swahili, etc.), unless mechanisms of choice as such are considered to be part of UG, which is not the standard position. The point is that linguistic knowledge is determined by the environment in a fundamental sense; obviously a child exposed to Italian learns only that language, never English, suggesting a rational-causal (rather than a brute-causal) relation of content between the data and the knowledge achieved (Atkinson 1987, Fodor 1981). Thus a nativist model which supposedly does not require some kind of learning component does not solve the puzzle of induction of languages; it simply buries the problem.

It is, then, plausible that the process of acquisition involves some (in part specialized) mechanisms that can quite legitimately be characterized as learning processes mediating the interactions between the environment and the innate knowledge. After all, as Levelt remarks, 'It is quite arbitrary to call some of these interactions learning and others not, the question becomes semantic, rather than empirical' (1974, vol. 3: 160). Language acquisition, in any case, involves the *learning* of a large number of purely arbitrary facts of an ambient language, perhaps well beyond the scope of variation defined by UG. The analogy with the growth of a physical organ clearly needs to be somewhat qualified. Broadly following this line of argument, one could posit that there is a learning theory associated with UG comprising some specialized, domain-specific learning principles, distinct from the ones used in general and designed to exploit experiential evidence within the constraints imposed by UG. A learning theory consisting of such specialized mechanisms is represented as LT_s in the following modified schema, where general learning principles also figure as LT_g.

(5) DATA   → $\boxed{LT_g + LT_s + UG}$ →   KNOWLEDGE OF LANGUAGE

Here domain-general inductive mechanisms are depicted as collaborating with UG and a specialized learning component in the acquisition of language, the implication being that such mechanisms are not entirely irrelevant to the acquisition of grammar, although for obvious reasons domain-specific learning principles must still be regarded as paramount (cf. Wexler and Culicover 1980: 5). In short, we wish to acknowledge the possibility that the UG-related learning principles and general learning procedures are not mutually exclusive in an absolute sense, or even that general mechanisms could actually be preprogrammed to aid the development of grammar (McCawley 1983).[6] These latter are almost certainly involved in the acquisition of idiosyncratic, language-particular facts, so that it should come as no surprise if it turns out that they are somehow implicated, presumably to a lesser extent, in the induction of (core) grammars as well. In any event, it is conceivable that a comprehensive learning theory for natural language, call it LT(L), may emerge only from the combination of LT_g, LT_s, and UG. Having said that, we would like to reemphasize that LT_g does not appear to be particularly crucial in explaining parameter fixation, and that its role in the acquisition of syntax may be restricted to the learning of certain peripheral aspects of the grammar of a language.[7]

1.3   A note on methodology

In line with the foregoing discussion, in this work we adopt a methodological perspective involving two key aspects of the human language learning system, namely Universal Grammar (UG), and a largely domain-specific learning theory. Also considered are some relevant data as reported in a number of developmental studies of child language acquisition (e.g. Radford 1990).

Clearly, one has to rely on some version of linguistic theory for a characterization of the specific nature of grammar. Our learnability perspective is firmly grounded in the theory of UG propounded by Chomsky and his followers (Chomsky 1981, and subsequent work), often referred to as the Government-Binding theory (GB) or the principles-and-parameters approach within current linguistic theory.[8] (This approach is outlined for reference in chapter 2 of this book.)

As we know, UG is construed by Chomsky as the characterization of the initial state of the child language learner, delimiting *what* can be learned when humans acquire language. In contrast, what we term learning theory strives to explain *how* language acquisition might take place. It comprises, among other things, the process of selection of syntactic knowledge, usually referred to as parameter setting or parameter fixation, whereby the child learner is hypothesized to identify the appropriate parameter values associated with the language to be learned (Atkinson 1987, Hyams 1986, Lightfoot 1989, Manzini and Wexler 1987, Piattelli-Palmarini 1989; also see the papers in Roca 1990, and Roeper and Williams 1987). As is obvious, the parameter-setting model is the procedural offshoot of the representational view known as the principles-and-parameters approach.

UG and learning theory are assumed to interact in order to bring about the process of acquisition, which gives rise to the knowledge of a particular language. The knowledge so acquired is manifested in the learner's linguistic behaviour at different stages of development, and is hence available, in some sense, as evidence of the occurrence of the process. Note that due to performance or maturation factors this evidence may not truly reflect the state of the knowledge at any given point in the course of acquisition. Nevertheless, we feel that learnability considerations should not ignore developmental evidence (cf. Pinker 1984; White 1981, 1982), though one should be mindful of the tenuous connection the latter might have with the actual knowledge-base in the mind, and should remember that representational change and behavioural change may not always go hand in hand (cf. Grimshaw and Rosen 1990, Karmiloff-Smith 1987).

2 The components of the linguistic system

This chapter focuses on the major components of Universal Grammar (UG), as conceived within the theory of principles-and-parameters. In addition to providing the general linguistic background, it describes the theory with an eye to those aspects of syntax which are particularly relevant to the present study. The theory comprises a lexical-categorial base, a set of connected levels of representation, various interpretive conventions and mechanisms, and a number of interacting subtheories constraining the overall system.

2.1 Projection and interpretation

The base projects lexical and categorial properties uniformly onto the representational levels, namely the syntactic levels of D-structure and S-structure, and the interpretive levels known as PF (phonological form) and LF (logical form). The lexicon contains items classifiable into two types of categories, lexical categories and functional categories. The former include A, N, V, and P, whereas the set of functional categories consists of Comp(lementizer) or C (head of CP = S'), Infl(ection) or I (head of IP = S), and Det(erminer); under some recent accounts (e.g. Chomsky 1989, Pollock 1989), T(ense), Agr(eement), and Neg (i.e. the negative particle) are further recognized as replacements for or additions to such categories.

Lexical items, particularly those belonging to major lexical categories, are associated with subcategorial frames depicting their *S(emantic)-selection* and *C(ategorial)-selection* properties (Grimshaw 1979, Pesetsky 1982). Syntactically active semantic properties of selecting elements are embodied in their θ-grids (Higginbotham 1985, Stowell 1981), i.e. the set of thematic (or θ-) roles they can assign. These θ-roles are mapped onto their *canonical structural realizations* (CSRs) (Chomsky 1986a, Grimshaw 1981). Thus the CSR of an S-selected category C, or CSR(C), will be an appropriate syntactic category or a set of such categories, as shown below

15

underlined elements depict subjects or external arguments, and the rest
complements or internal arguments (cf. Williams 1981b).

(1) a.i *hit*: V, ⟨agent, goal⟩
      CSR (agent, goal) = NP, NP
   ii *convince*: V, ⟨agent, goal, proposition⟩
      CSR (agent, goal, proposition) = NP, NP, CP
  b.i [$_{NP}$ He] hit [$_{NP}$ John]
   ii [$_{NP}$ He] convinced [$_{NP}$ John] [$_{CP}$ that he should go to the cinema]

Arguments appear in *A-positions*, i.e. the subject and object positions.
Nonargument positions, such as those occupied by complementizers, verbs
or adjuncts, are known as A′ (A-bar)-positions. θ-roles are assigned by
lexical categories directly, i.e. under strict sisterhood, to the internal
arguments, whereas the θ-roles of arguments in the subject or Spec(ifier)
position may be selected compositionally, i.e. through the mediation of a
higher level projection; hence the term external argument. Thus while a V
internally assigns a θ-role to an object, the subject gets its θ-role indirectly
from the VP. Alternatively, subjects may be considered to originate VP-
internally in an adjoined position, where they receive their θ-role from VP
under sisterhood, and then move to the sentence-initial position for reasons
of Case (e.g. see Fukui 1986, Manzini 1989).

The direct selection of complements is enforced by an overarching
constraint on the levels of representation, stated below in a basic form.

(2) *The Projection Principle*
    Configurations at each representational level are projected from the
    lexicon in keeping with the selectional properties of lexical items.

The indirect selection of the subject of a sentence is governed by *the
Extended Projection Principle* (Chomsky 1982) or by a predication rule
(Rothstein 1983, Williams 1980),[1] requiring that clauses or predicates have
subjects. Optionally NPs may also have subjects, typically in the form of
another genitive NP. In the case of clauses the requirement to have a subject
is so strong that it is fulfilled even in case of the nonavailability of a
referential subject, namely by the insertion of a *pleonastic* or *expletive*
subject.

The lexicon has come to acquire a considerably important role in the
determination of syntactic properties at various levels of representation.
The correspondence between the selectional properties of words and the
specific syntactic structures projected from them, though poorly understood, is nontrivial, a fact of great potential importance in language

acquisition since it might mean that the task of learning a language could be reduced to the identification of such lexical properties as are deducible from the meanings of lexical items in some plausible manner (Chomsky 1986a). The assumption, of course, is that the child can come to know the meaning of words by largely nonlinguistic means, and that the syntactic system is then bootstrapped through the semantic information so acquired (see Pinker 1984, 1987, 1989, Wexler and Culicover 1980, on this and related issues).[2]

Just as the Projection Principle is a general constraint on syntactic representations, *the Full Interpretation Principle* (strictly speaking, perhaps not yet so concretely defined as to deserve the status of a UG principle, as Chomsky 1989 points out; but cf. Kempson 1988) is a global condition on their interpretation in the LF and PF components. This principle can be stated in the following form, adapted from Chomsky (1986a).

(3) *The Full Interpretation Principle*
Every element must receive an appropriate interpretation in the interpretive components (i.e. LF and PF).

Appropriate interpretation presupposes the notion of *licensing*, which subsumes some (often overlapping) grammatical processes, such as those pertaining to projection, government, etc. Chomsky writes that 'Every element that appears in a well-formed structure must be *licensed* in one of a small number of available ways' (1986a: 93). Thus a V which θ-marks an object under government licenses that object, and so forth. In general the Projection Principle, the Extended Projection Principle, and some other related principles (e.g. the Empty Category Principle, or ECP for short; see section 2.3.3 below) play a crucial role in licensing, and the Full Interpretation Principle and other conceptual (assignment of reference, etc.) and syntactic (e.g. feature agreement, coindexation, binding, etc.) interpretive mechanisms make it certain that every licensed element acquires an interpretation. In other words licensing encapsulates the grammatical *raison d'être* of an element. Provided that this sort of syntactic reason is available for the presence of every element, then and only then will it be subjected to full interpretation.

A number of important issues in the theory relate to how the empty categories (ECs) are licensed and interpreted. Interestingly, like phonetically overt categories these too are licensed by virtue of the (Extended) Projection Principle – which requires that a subcategorized position, whether lexicalized or phonetically empty, should be present at all levels –

and the ECP, and interpreted differently by means of a variety of (co)referential mechanisms. The ones typically identified are: NP-trace, the trace of a moved NP; Wh-trace, the variable/trace left by a moved Wh-phrase; PRO, the abstract subject of a nonfinite clause; and *pro*, the phonologically null subject of finite sentences, which is found in pro-drop languages. While the pattern of occurrence of PRO is more or less uniform across various languages, whether a language can have a phonetically null subject in tensed clauses (i.e. *pro*) is determined by the null-subject parameter (see section 2.4 below).

As implied above, the architecture of linguistic meaning is partly syntactic and partly conceptual. Take the case of nominal expressions as an example. Nominal expressions either directly denote 'objects' in the mental domain (sometimes called 'D') serving as the interface between the lexicon and the conceptual system (Bouchard 1984, Chomsky 1981, Montalbetti and Wexler 1985), or they are coreferential with another denoting expression, namely an antecedent. Any expression referring to a mental object in D is said to be coindexed with that object, and the index thus acquired by the lexical item is termed its *R(eferential)-index* (Bouchard 1984). Such a lexical item is an *R(eferential)-expression*, in contrast with an expression which is *referentially dependent* on an antecedent from which it picks up its R-index. The class of R-expressions principally includes names and variables; among the referentially dependent elements anaphors, traces of moved elements, and bound pronouns figure prominently.

2.2   Levels of representation and movement

The levels provide the structural foundations for the transformational and interpretive rules. Transformational movement connects the various levels of representation, i.e. D-structure, S-structure, PF and LF. D-structure is purely a structural manifestation of θ-grids. For each legitimate θ-role a θ-position is projected. An A-position may or may not be a θ-position; if not then it will count as a θ' *(θ-bar)-position*. To illustrate, pleonastic subjects appear in θ'-positions (which are nevertheless A-positions). Syntactic movement takes place between D-structure and S-structure, during which D-structure is uniquely mapped onto S-structure by means of the general rule 'Move α', which says move anything anywhere. NP-movement and Wh-movement (see 4a–b respectively) are the two major types of movement that may occur in syntax.

(4)a. John$_i$ was sacked t_i
   b. Who$_i$ did John hit t_i?

An important consequence of movement is the formation of discontinuous elements, or *chains*, which are expressed by means of coindexing, as illustrated in (4). A phrase that moves to an A-position forms an *A-chain* with its trace; NP-movement from the θ-marked object position of a passive verb to the Case-marked subject position of the clause is an example of this type of chain (4a). Correspondingly, a phrase that lands in a nonargument position results in the creation of an A'-chain, an example of which is provided by Wh-movement (4b).[3]

S-structure is dually mapped onto PF and LF. PF is the interface between the syntax and one aspect of the system of language use; it constitutes what is phonetically realized; and LF, the interface between the syntax and the logico-semantic systems of the mind, contributes to semantic interpretation and thus in part determines how a sentence is to be understood (May 1985). There is no intermapping between PF and LF and thus whatever goes on at LF is not 'visible' to PF and *vice versa*; see (5) for a schematic representation.

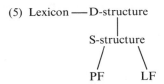

(5) Lexicon —— D-structure

S-structure

PF   LF

LF movement is universal; all quantifiers move at LF for scopal reasons, and Wh-phrases do the same if they have not already done so in the syntax. But syntactic movement is subject to variation: thus, whether or not Wh-movement is allowed between D-structure and S-structure is parameterized, with English having movement in syntax, and Chinese and Japanese having no syntactic Wh-movement (see Aoun et al. 1987, Chomsky 1986b, Lasnik and Saito 1984 for further detail).

Structurally, there are two major kinds of movement, substitution and adjunction. Substitution can comprise the movement of maximal projections or heads: in the case of the former a complement (a maximal projection) moves to occupy a canonical X-bar position (i.e. Spec of CP, IP, etc.); both NP-movement and Wh-movement are examples of this type of substitution; the other type of substitution is head-to-head movement, or simply head movement, exemplified by the movement of V into Infl to acquire tense and agreement (Agr) features which are based in Infl, or the movement of an auxiliary verb from Infl to Comp. It is noteworthy that the phenomenon explained above in terms of V-movement was traditionally characterized as an affixation process, or a local morphological movement rule, called Rule-R in Chomsky (1981), during which tense and grammatical features (ϕ-features) were considered to be instantiated on the uninflected verbal stem.

2.3   The subtheories

The network of subtheories or modules of UG, which interact among themselves to yield the core grammar of a particular language, are briefly described one by one in the following pages.

2.3.1   X-bar theory

This subtheory deals with the phrasal projections of various categories and determines the level ($X°$, X', or $X''=XP$) of constituent structure, essentially in accordance with the following configurational schemata, where X ranges over different types of categories, ' and " depict bar levels, and * indicates that the repeated occurrence of any of the phrases so marked is possible.

(6) $X'=X\ XP*$
$XP=XP*\ X'$

The order of various constituents, however, is parameterized and is handled independently by the head-direction parameter (Huang 1982), and by the parameters determining the direction of θ-role and Case assignment (Koopman 1984, Travis 1984). To illustrate, the direction in which a complement can occur is decided by the head-direction parameter. Thus a language may be head-first (English, 7a), or head-last (Hindi–Urdu, 7b), a variation illustrated here with respect to V.

(7)a. He bought a book
　　　　V　→　NP
　 b. Us　ne　kitaab khariidii
　　　　(S)he　Erg book　bought
　　　　　　 NP　←　V

Maximal projections ($XP=NP$, VP, IP, etc.) may contain a Spec(ifier) and one or more complements in addition to the head ($X°=N$, V, I, etc.), whereas intermediate projections ($X'=N'$, V', etc.) may only contain the complement(s), if any, as shown in (8).

(8)
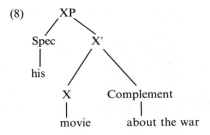

On the analysis proposed in Stowell (1981) and adopted in Chomsky (1986b; also see Koopman 1984, Travis 1984), functional categories as well as lexical categories participate in a uniform two-bar system, as illustrated in (9), where, as in (8), the order and other detail are for English.

(9)

Even more articulated versions of X-bar syntax have been proposed incorporating further phrasal projections, e.g. T(ense)P, Agr(eement)P (each independently headed by one of the twin components of IP), and NegP (see Pollock 1989, Chomsky 1989).[4]

The X-bar system is fundamental to the theory, because it generates licit structural configurations which enter into the definitions of principles and parameters contained in all the subtheories. One such configuration, defined in (10), is known as *c-command*, which is involved in the conception of several important constructs of the theory, e.g. government and binding (see the definitions in sections 2.3.3 and 2.3.7).

> (10) *C-command*
> α c-commands β iff α does not dominate β and every branching node that dominates α dominates β.

Just as configurations like c-command are stated as necessary preconditions for various syntactic relations to operate, some others, e.g. maximal projections, are held to block them. In the latter case they are referred to as *barriers*. The notion of barrier is defined in Chomsky (1986b) in terms which are not purely structural, but crucially dependent on lexical elements involved and the attendant selectional properties.

2.3.2   θ-theory

The assignment of θ-roles, or θ-marking, affects all thematically relevant positions (or θ-positions). θ-roles are assigned at D-structure to NPs that are referential *arguments*, and checked at LF. θ-role assignment obeys the following global constraint.

> (11) *The θ-criterion*
> Each argument α appears in a chain containing a unique θ-position P, and each θ-position P appears in a chain containing a unique argument α.

Intuitively, the θ-criterion says that each argument bears one and only one θ-role, and each θ-role is assigned to one and only one argument. Like the Projection Principle, the θ-criterion applies at all levels of syntax, ensuring uniformity of θ-role assignment throughout.

2.3.3   Theory of government

The relation of *government* is tighter than c-command, and may be defined as follows (Chomsky 1986b, cf. Aoun and Sportiche 1983);

> (12) *Government*
> α governs β iff α c-commands β, and every barrier for β dominates α.

where $\alpha = X^\circ$, in the sense of X-bar theory, and for simplicity barrier may be taken to mean a maximal projection (see Chomsky 1986b for a more technical definition). As a rule Case and θ-role assignment occur under government. A special type of government is proper government (Chomsky 1986b, also see Lasnik and Saito 1984).

(13) *Proper government*
   α properly governs β iff α θ-governs or antecedent-governs β.

θ-government is equivalent to what is sometimes called lexical government (i.e. government by N, V, A, P), and antecedent government to coindexing with an antecedent. But notice that under some approaches the set of proper governors is said to be parameterized, which may additionally include functional categories Infl or Comp. So Huang (1982) claims that Infl is a proper governor in Chinese, and on Travis's (1984) analysis Comp is a proper governor in German.

Proper government functions as a precondition for extraction and is required for the licensing of empty categories in general (excepting PRO, and perhaps *pro* as well). The role of proper government in extraction is exhibited in English by the effect of the so-called *that*-trace Filter (i.e. *[*that*-t]), as exemplified in (14); (14a) is ill-formed because the position of the moved subject is not properly governed, since Infl does not count as a proper governor; on the other hand in (14b) the extraction site is governed by a lexical category, i.e. the verb, hence the creation of an EC by movement is legitimate.

(14)a. *Who$_i$ do you think [$_{CP}$ t$_i$′ [$_C$ that] [$_{IP}$ [$_{NP}$ t$_i$] came]]
    b. Who$_i$ do you think [$_{CP}$ t$_i$′ [$_C$ that] [$_{IP}$ Mary saw [$_{NP}$ t$_i$]]]

This constraining role of proper government is captured by what is known as the Empty Category Principle (ECP), which may be stated in the following manner.

(15) *The Empty Category Principle*
   An EC, particularly a trace, must be properly governed.

The ECP determines whether or not an empty category is permissible in a particular position.

2.3.4   Case theory

Abstract Case is an important phenomenon that interacts with mechanisms like the assignment of θ-roles and A-chain formation. The subject of a tensed clause is assigned nominative Case by the Infl, by virtue of the presence in the latter of tense and/or Agr, or by the presence in it of a raised verb (Koopman 1984). The object of a verb or a preposition is assigned objective or accusative Case, and an NP is assigned genitive Case in the context [$_{NP}$—N′]. Thus tensed Infl, V and P are all Case assigners: N, A and the infinitival Infl do not assign Case. The major tenet within the subtheory is a well-formedness condition, called *the Case Filter*, which operates at S-structure.

(16) *The Case Filter*
      Every phonetically overt NP must be Case-marked.

Excepting Wh-traces, all ECs may appear without Case; in fact, the Filter can be extended to mean that the overt realization of an NP at PF is made obligatory because of Case.

Recall that NP-traces are part of chains headed by Case-marked NPs; the θ-marked NPs move to the Case-marked positions in order to acquire Case, as they cannot get Case in their base-generated positions. See (4a) for an example; as the passive morphology on a verb renders it incapable of Case assignment, the object NP must undergo a process of 'function-changing' (Baker 1988), and move to the subject position. This explains why chains are headed by Case-marked elements and terminate in θ-marked positions; movement is never to a θ-position because that would result in a violation of the θ-criterion.

Further, an NP is rendered 'visible' for θ-marking only if it has Case (with the exception of PRO). A proper formulation of this condition, termed *the Visibility Condition*, might make (16) unnecessary, as it seems to yield more or less the same consequences (Chomsky 1986a: 94–5). The following statement of the condition, adapted from Chomsky (1986a, cf. Aoun 1985, Baker 1988, Fabb 1984) will be sufficient for our immediate purposes (see note 3 for an illustration of the linking referred to here).

(17) *Visibility Condition*
      A noun phrase can receive a θ-role only if it is in a position to which Case is assigned, or is linked to such a position.

It might as well be pointed out that a different view of the condition is taken in chapter 6.

2.3.5   Bounding theory

Bounding theory deals with subjacency restrictions on syntactic movement, setting bounds on how far an element can move from its original D-structure position. A somewhat dated version of the theory goes like this: generally no more than one bounding node can be crossed, but languages vary in their choice of what is to count as a bounding node. English, for instance, has NP and S as the bounding nodes, whereas Italian chooses NP and S′ (Rizzi 1982). Generally speaking, movement across more than one bounding node results in rapid deterioration of grammaticality, the reasons for which can be shown to follow from a theory of barriers (see Chomsky 1986b).

2.3.6 Control theory

PRO, the phonologically null subject of infinitival and gerundive clauses, acquires its referential content by means of a special indexing relation called *control*, which is not subject to c-command. The core case of control is obligatory coindexing with an antecedent, that is with the subject (18a) or object (18b) of the matrix clause; it is in this sense that PRO is held to be anaphoric. PRO is also pronominal because it can have independent (arbitrary) reference (18c).

(18)a. John$_i$ wanted [PRO$_i$ to sell the house]
    b. John persuaded Bill$_i$ [PRO$_i$ to sell the house]
    c. It is illegal [PRO$_{arb}$ to travel without a valid ticket]

2.3.7 Binding theory

In binding theory four categories of nominal expressions are established on the basis of the features ±anaphor and ±pronominal.

(19)a. [+anaphor, −pronominal]
    b. [−anaphor, +pronominal]
    c. [+anaphor, +pronominal]
    d. [−anaphor, −pronominal]

(19a) denotes anaphors (reflexives, reciprocals, NP-traces), (19b) pronominals (lexical pronouns, *pro*), (19c) the pronominal anaphor PRO, and (19d) R-expressions (names and variables). Chomsky (1981) proposed the following three principles of binding.

(20) *Binding principles*
    A. An anaphor is bound in its governing category.
    B. A pronominal is free in its governing category.
    C. An R-expression is free.

The hypothesis that PRO is ungoverned (so-called 'PRO theorem') is considered to fall out of these principles, as being a pronominal anaphor it should be subject to both principles A and B at the same time; hence it is stipulated that PRO is ungoverned and thus does not possess a governing category; this view, as will be discussed in chapter 6, has been challenged by many (e.g. Borer 1989, Bouchard 1984, Hornstein and Lightfoot 1987, Huang 1989, Manzini 1983).

Binding theory emerges from the intersection of coreference and c-command; cases of coreference without c-command do not fall within its purview. Therefore technically *binding* means being coindexed with a c-commanding antecedent; thus:

> (21) *Binding*
> α binds β iff
> a. α and β are coindexed, and
> b. α c-commands β.

A governing category, typically an NP or an S, is defined in (22), along with the related definitions of the notion of accessibility (23) and a condition on indexing (24).

> (22) *Governing category*
> γ is a governing category for α iff
> γ is the minimal category containing α, a governor for α, and a subject accessible to α.
>
> (23) *Accessibility*
> α is accessible to β iff
> a. α c-commands β, and
> b. coindexing of α and β does not violate the i-within-i condition.
>
> (24) *The i-within-i condition*
> $*[_\delta \ldots \alpha \ldots]$, where δ and α bear the same index.

Binding principles explain the following contrasts.

> (25)a.   John believes that [Mary$_i$ has bought herself$_i$ a new cap]
> *Mary$_i$ believes that [John has bought herself$_i$ a new cap]
> b. *John believes that [Mary$_i$ has bought her$_i$ a new cap]
> Mary$_i$ believes that [John has bought her$_i$ a new cap]
> c. *John believes that [she$_i$ has bought Mary$_i$ a new cap]
> *She$_i$ believes that [John has bought Mary$_i$ a new cap]

The square brackets indicate the respective governing categories. (25a) shows that anaphors must be bound in their governing category. On the other hand, pronominals tend to avoid being bound locally. In other words, for pronominals disjoint reference is required in a designated governing category, though they may be bound to an antecedent outside it (see 25b). Finally, (25c) demonstrates that denoting expressions must not be bound at all.

In contrast with the unitary accounts (Chomsky 1981, Manzini 1983), under some analyses binding is parameterized (Koster 1984, Manzini and Wexler 1987, Wexler and Manzini 1987, Yang 1984). In particular, Wexler and Manzini claim that the notion of governing category may vary under a five-valued parameter, with the least marked value being associated with the simplest type of governing category and the smallest language (see chapter 4 for detail).[5]

2.4   Null subjects: the case of a parameter

It is well known that null definite pronouns are optionally allowed in the subject position of tensed clauses in some languages, e.g. Italian, Spanish, Chinese, Japanese, Hindi–Urdu, etc. In the sentences containing null subjects, the subject position is now almost universally considered (following Chomsky 1982) to be occupied by the empty category *pro*. The following Italian (26a – from Chomsky 1981) and Hindi–Urdu (26b) constructions illustrate the phenomenon, which is attributed to the null-subject parameter.

(26)a. [$_{NP}$ e] ho trovato il libro
  '(I) found the book'
  b. [$_{NP}$ e] kitaab dhõõd lii
  '(I, etc.) found the book'

Traditionally, null subjects are believed to be licensed by the presence of rich verbal inflection reflecting agreement with the subject (since Taraldsen 1978), and/or by a requirement of proper government (e.g. Chomsky 1981, 1982, Rizzi 1982). Further, the parameter is traditionally considered to have two contrasting values, allowing languages with and without null-subject sentences. An interesting part of the research is devoted to language acquisition (e.g. Hyams 1986, Radford 1990, Valian 1990), and offers an insightful perspective involving the interaction of linguistic and acquisitional points of view (see chapters 4 and 5 for detail).

The following are two of the properties often alleged to be typical of the null-subject languages.

(27)a. The subject may be freely inverted in simple sentences.
  b. Wh-movement in apparent violation of the *that*-trace Filter may occur.

These are considered to be systematically interrelated, in keeping with the rich deductive structure of UG envisaged by Chomsky (1981). Chomsky (1981) suggests that pro-drop is possible basically when Infl, especially its

Agr component, is pronominal in character. He further suggests that this correlation may show up in the form of overt inflection on the verb. Chomsky (1981) outlines two proposals with regard to the null-subject parameter, one of which relies on the assumption that, in contrast to non-pro-drop languages, Infl/Agr is a proper governor in pro-drop languages. In line with this viewpoint, the parameter may be formulated as in (28)

(28) Infl may (not) be a proper governor.

The pro-drop languages have the option of having an empty pronominal in the subject position because this empty position can be properly governed by Agr, satisfying the Empty Category Principle. Besides, when Agr is a proper governor the *that*-trace effect is eliminated because the empty position no longer needs to be properly governed from any pre-S position, a process that would be blocked by a lexically filled Comp.

The second proposal is based on the hypothesis that in null-subject languages Infl cannot properly govern the empty subject position, which consequently need not be governed and is occupied by PRO (cf. Jaeggli 1982). This proposal formulates the parameter in terms of Rule-R, a PF affixation rule that moves Infl-based tense and agreement features to the end of the verbal stem. Chomsky says that in pro-drop languages Rule-R has the option of applying in syntax as well as in PF. When it applies in syntax, it removes Infl from its D-structure position from where it governed the subject position and thus required the subject to be lexicalized. The idea is that in languages like English and French Rule-R always applies in PF, so that PRO cannot appear in the subject position in tensed clauses since this position is always governed at the appropriate levels of representation; recall that the usual assumption is that PRO must never be governed. On the other hand, in pro-drop languages like Italian, as a result of Rule-R the Infl may move in the syntax to a postverbal position, from where it can no longer govern the subject position, but can instead govern and Case-mark a postposed subject. Chomsky (1981) states the parameter as in (29).

(29) Rule-R may apply in the syntax.

Rizzi (1982), assuming the null-subject position to be occupied by a properly governed empty category, claims that even in pro-drop languages like Italian the *that*-trace effect holds; under Rizzi's account pro-drop languages obey the ECP in general, just like the non-pro-drop languages. His argument is that in Italian the long Wh-extraction of a subject is from a postverbal position, as illustrated here (but see Picallo 1984 for a contrary view based on Catalan data).

(30) wh$_i$ ... [$_S$ [$_{NP}$ e$_i$] Infl [$_{VP}$ [$_{VP}$ V ...] [$_{NP}$ e$_i$]]]

Judging from the above accounts, it seems likely that the possibilities of the occurrence of null and inverted subjects could be inextricably linked. However, Safir (1985) argues that the two properties emanate from two different parameters (also cf. Jaeggli and Safir 1989a), a view which is also assumed in Hyams (1986). If such a view is plausible, then four different types of language will be predicted. The first type is exemplified by English and French, which may be classified as −Inversion and −Null Subject; Italian (Rizzi 1982), Spanish (Jaeggli and Safir 1989a) and the Bani Hassan dialect of Arabic (Kenstowicz 1989) fall into the second category, which can be described as +Inversion and +Null Subject. The two remaining combinations also appear to be attested: Portuguese (Chao 1980, Safir 1985), Irish (Travis 1984), Japanese (Kilby 1987), and Chinese (Safir, p.c.) fit the third type (−Inversion and +Null Subject), as they are pro-drop, but in general do not allow subject postposing. Finally, according to Safir (1985), the fourth type (+Inversion and −Null Subject) is represented by Northern Italian dialects Modenese and Trentino, which permit postverbal subjects, but not empty ones.

So perhaps all the logical combinations of pro-drop and subject inversion are indeed found in existing languages. However, Rizzi (1986b) and Brandi and Cordin (1989) argue that Northern Italian dialects, exemplifying the class of languages crucial to the existence of the fourth type, are in fact null-subject languages. They maintain that the apparent subject clitic in these Italian dialects actually represents the agreement component of Infl, as it may cooccur with a lexical subject, and is thus different from the subject clitic of a non-null-subject language like French. However, even if it can be shown that the fourth type is non-existent, it would only amount to the claim that languages which are pro-drop need not have obligatory subject inversion, but that the converse is not true; as for the third type (e.g. Portuguese, Japanese, Chinese, etc.), clearly the pro-drop is both 'theoretically and empirically independent' of the free inversion of subjects (Jaeggli and Safir 1989a).[6]

3 *The components of the learning system*

Having outlined the patterns of interaction between UG and the learning theory, and described the essentials of the former, it may be beneficial now to begin to establish the basis of a systematic theory of language acquisition. The following pages, consequently, are intended to lay down the groundwork of such a theory.

3.1   Foundations of the learning theory

The primary goal of the learning theory is to study every component of the phenomenon of language learning methodically, e.g. the learner, the nature of the input data, the object of learning, etc. To this end we informally adopt the concept of a *learning paradigm* from Osherson, Stob and Weinstein (1984, 1986a). We now introduce this concept, which will be employed throughout as the overarching framework for the discussion of various aspects of learnability.

A learning paradigm includes, to begin with, some explicit characterization of what is learned: e.g. the grammar of the language to be learned, described in accordance with a viable theory of natural language. Further, it contains a view of how something is learned (i.e. a set of learning mechanisms), by whom (i.e. information about the nature of the learner), and under what conditions (i.e. some specific view of the nature and complexity of the experience required as input to the learning system). In short, we adapt the following definition of a learning paradigm from Osherson et al. (1986a: 7):

(1) A *learning paradigm* means any precise rendition of the basic concepts of learning.

As to the basic concepts of learning, Osherson et al. (1986a: 7) identify these:

(2)a. a learner
    b. a thing to be learned

   c. an environment in which the thing to be learned is exhibited to the learner

   d. the hypotheses that occur to the learner about the thing to be learned on the basis of the environment

To these an associated *criterion of success* is further added, which defines when learning should be considered successful. The most straightforward criterion is this: the learner is said to be successful when his or her hypotheses about the thing to be learned achieve compatibility with the exhibited data in some finite time, and thereafter remain stable and accurate. A learning paradigm, in other words, is a systematic and somewhat idealized representation of the empirical conditions under which a particular type of learning takes place. In the light of the foregoing discussion, this is how learning theory is conceptualized by Osherson et al. (1986a: 7):

   (3) *Learning theory* is the study of learning paradigms.

3.1.1 The role of idealizations

Perhaps the most important aspect of a learning paradigm – whether it is explicit, as in formal models (see section 3.2), or implicit, as is more usual – is the extent to which the components assumed to be a part of the learning system are empirically verifiable. For simplification and ease of analysis, though, researchers often, at least to begin with, resort to various idealizations, and are content with essentially correct but partial accounts of the learner, the object of learning, the environment, etc. As we know, within a learnability framework it is customary to abstract away from different kinds of developmental and maturational factors. To be more concrete, let us take the case of the learner's environment by way of illustration.

In the reductive system of analysis under study, an environment may be defined as a set of isolated examples presented to the learner, in principle not denying the bootstrapping role of a meaningful context, but, in actual practice, disregarding the detail of this role (see Pinker 1987, 1989 for attempts to address this issue). Further, these examples are generally considered to be well-formed, only worthy of the ideal speaker–hearer, although some researchers do attempt to deal with the effects of 'noisy data', e.g. Valian (1989, 1990), who considers the role of 'clipped' subjectless sentences in the acquisition of the null-subject phenomenon (also see Osherson et al. 1984, 1986a, for a formal perspective on the question of noisy data). An often unstated belief, methodologically convenient but not necessarily correct, is that the child learner can, somehow, distinguish good examples from bad ones, and that he or she only focuses on the former. In point of fact, environmental input can be misleading in several respects; for instance it may contain:

(4)a. performance errors (e.g. those due to slips of the tongue, lapses of memory, mental strain, etc.)
b. ungrammatical strings (e.g. those spoken by a linguistically deficient informant)
c. apparently contradictory information about the input language (e.g. that resulting from stylistic variation, superficial inconsistency in the grammar, etc.)
d. examples from different social and regional dialects, even from entirely different languages

and so forth, not to mention the inverse possibility that the input may *not* exhibit certain perfectly grammatical examples which are rarely used.

The point is that it does not seem too reasonable to try to be very realistic; as in physical sciences, the best way to understand the reality appears to be that of cautioning against overelaboration, encouraging, instead, a piecemeal but orderly and sharpened mode of inquiry. Idealizations, consequently, are bound to be a part of a learnability-theoretic approach to language acquisition. That, in fact, is one of the reasons why, while addressing various issues, we need to keep in mind a specified learning paradigm, so that we know in advance in what respects it is partial or deficient, and therefore merits only the amount of credibility built into it as a matter of conscious design – no more, no less.

Learnability theory, it appears then, is an approach to the study of acquisition that is more or less formal, or is at least systematic, in the sense that it takes into account some explicit learning paradigm; further, it is based on clearly stated idealizations, of course with the ultimate aim of being able to gradually move away from these idealizations and approximate towards actual conditions of learning.

3.1.2   Learning mechanisms

The emergence of language may involve several (interweaved) modes of acquisition, yielding at least these three basic types, sequenced in the ascending order of the amount of 'learning' involved.

(5)a. Maturation
b. Selective learning
c. Observational learning

Maturation is, by definition, a 'no-learning' mechanism, and denotes change emanating from genotype at a pre-specified time in consequence of neurological growth. Abstractly, this could be exemplified by the putative development of linguistic principles (Borer and Wexler 1987, 1988; Radford 1990, Wexler 1989). Selective learning represents change *prima facie* induced by environment but nevertheless constrained genetically, and therefore operating within prescribed limits. It may be revealed as parameter fixation triggered by relevant input (Lightfoot 1989, Piattelli-Palmarini 1986, 1989, Roeper and Williams 1987). Finally, learning strategies that are, apparently, independent of any specific cognitive system, and crucially depend upon the learner's close inspection of the environmental input, fall into the category of observational learning. Observation of the frequency of occurrence of certain forms, or for that matter of the consistency of their nonoccurrence, and in fact any other modes involving some sifting of evidence, are examples of this mechanism (Lasnik 1990, Oehrle 1985, Valian 1989).

(5a) and (5b) may define the crux of the matter; at the very least they constitute a convenient and simplifying methodological reduction. Although (5c) is notoriously difficult to understand, even more difficult to study in the first place, we suspect that its explanatory potential may not be inconsiderable.

3.1.3 Evidence and triggers

Evidence is that component of a learning system which is external to the learner, who, consequently, may not be able to exercise much control over it. Three fundamental issues will need to be addressed by any theory of evidence:

(6)a. the extent to which environmental evidence has a role in the learning process: that is, how much of the learning process is amenable to experiential manipulation
  b. the kind of evidence required for a particular case of learning (positive, negative, etc.)
  c. the identification and nature of special elements of evidence (known as triggers) that may be more effective than others for a given purpose: that is, how frequent and complex the triggers need to be, etc.

The first issue (6a) can be easily related to the typology of learning mechanisms postulated above. As far as maturation is concerned, the role of evidential input has to be minimal, even to the point of being nonexistent in some, or most, cases. Parametric selection, however, will depend on input within some well-defined limits, providing an opportunity for a fine-grained study of the interaction of the input and the acquisition. And, finally, in observational learning the role of evidence will be greater, though perhaps less clearly definable in several cases.

Coming to the second issue (6b), primarily evidence may be positive or negative; descriptions of these, and also their derivative or indirect forms, will appear below in due course.

Finally, triggers (6c) are supposed to constitute a (small) subset of the child's total environmental input. The important observations regarding these are that: (a) they must be salient enough to be recognizable as triggers whenever they are to be utilized; (b) their degree of complexity may be an important variable in relation to particular forms to be acquired, or in accordance with the learner's maturational capacities; (c) the time of their utilization by the learner, or their relative frequency, or both, may matter; (d) their effect may be unique, i.e. one-to-one, or they might have a 'ripple effect' (Buckingham 1989), influencing several parts of grammar at the same time; and, (e) triggers of obligatory structures may be more readily available than their optional counterparts, in which case the latter might have to be induced on the basis of criteria of frequency or pragmatic necessity, or conceivably both, as often these two aspects happen to be interdependent.

In general, it is assumed that evidence (a) should at least be available, and at most be appropriately frequent, (b) should be simple enough to be processed easily by the learner's inchoate knowledge and performance abilities, (c) should be sufficiently meaningful; i.e. semantically well-formed, intellectually simple enough, and pragmatically facilitative, (d) should not rely heavily on 'counting' procedures, but presumably in cases pertaining to observational learning such procedures will most probably be relevant, and (e) should contain crucial triggers of suitable complexity, not depending a great deal for their impact, arguably not at all, on any type of negative feedback.

3.1.4   Learning by example

It ought to be pointed out that the conception of learning under consideration is a special one. It may be called 'learning by example', in contrast with 'learning by instruction', and is characterized by presentation of examples without much explicit information about them. Suppose there is a language L, then maximally the learner may be presented with two disjoint finite sets S and T of examples such that S ⊆ L and T ⊆ L', where L' is the complement of L, containing negative data, i.e. examples *not* included in L. S is usually known as positive data, and is a special case of presentation by example when T is empty. When T is not empty the negative information is supplied in addition; thus for any datum *s* it is indicated whether *s* ∈ L or not. Later we go into greater detail about the different forms exemplification can take.

Learning by positive example is generally considered to be the primary mode of language acquisition; it is further held that negative examples are either not available to the learner at all (Baker 1979, Brown and Hanlon 1970), or if sporadically accessible, the learner does not respond to them in any significant way (Braine 1971, McNeill 1966); beyond any doubt, negative information is never presented exhaustively, as conceived in formal studies such as Gold (1967). Then how does the learner succeed in conjecturing the correct grammar? We presume he or she can do so if he possesses an inherent evaluation procedure for the hypotheses that occur to him; the procedure will bias the learner's choice of hypotheses from the very start, and eventually make him choose the correct set of hypotheses. A learner equipped with an evaluation procedure should not be in danger of having to inspect a large number of hypotheses; as Chomsky states, 'It must be, then, that the "guessing instinct" submits very few admissible hypotheses to the evaluation procedure' (1986a: 55).

3.1.5 Learning problems

Considering its relative ease, speed and regularity, language learning by the child is no doubt a feat of some magnitude. But that does not mean it is without its problems.

A familiar issue in the theory of learnability is *the overgeneralization problem* (Baker 1979, Bowerman 1987, Dell 1981, Lasnik 1981, Pinker 1986, 1989, Williams 1981a; also see several papers in MacWhinney 1987). The problem can arise if the learner makes too large a conjecture, and if the correct hypothesis happens to be included in the conjecture arrived at. In such an event the learner might always be stuck with the wrong guess, as every datum will be compatible with both the more inclusive and the less inclusive guesses, ruling out the possibility of disconfirmation of the incorrect hypothesis from positive examples. But children almost invariably succeed in developing correct grammars. Suppose that children do indeed overgeneralize, the question then arises: how do they ever manage to accomplish the enormously difficult unlearning task required of them? The traditional answer to this puzzle, in keeping with the 'no negative evidence' assumption mentioned previously, is that the child language learner is conservative by nature and does not overgeneralize at all; he always conjectures the narrowest hypothesis first, and changes his mind only if positive evidence to the contrary is provided. The conservatism hypothesis was first described explicitly by Baker (1979) in connection with the learning of the dative alternation in English.

However, it has been shown, contrary to Baker's (1979) prediction, that English-speaking children do operate with some kind of nonconservative lexical redundancy rule which is formulated on grounds of analogy and consequently induces inappropriate generalizations of dativization (Mazurkewich and White 1984, Pinker 1989, Randall 1985). Some examples drawn from Mazurkewich and White (1984) are reproduced below; these sentences were incorrectly judged to be grammatical by their subjects (age approximately 9–15 years). The examples under (7a) are those of *to*-datives, those under (7b) of *for*-datives.

(7)a. *David suggested Ruth the trip
      *Susan explained Jane the problem
      *Bob reported the police the incident
   b. *Anne created Sarah a costume
      *Tom captured Canada the prize
      *Paul designed Claire a house

Now overgeneralization is just one of the many predicaments in which the child may find himself, though by general consensus it is the most serious one. There are other ways for the child to use the environmental evidence with results that would not be entirely consistent with the adult grammar. Let us therefore try to outline the relationships that may exist between the learner's (provisional or intermediate) hypotheses at any given time during the learning process and the adult grammar.

First suppose that the target grammar G has an element 'a', whereas the learner's grammar !G has another competing form '*b' which does not exist in G, as indicated by the prefixed star; that is, G and !G are disjoint with respect to the forms 'a' and '*b' (see (i), table 1). This is an example of what may be called *the substitution problem*, since the learner has made the wrong generalization, resulting in the substitution of '*b' for 'a'. A simple example is the use of *goed* instead of *went* as the past tense form of the verb *go*, an obvious result of the incorrect generalization of the use of the suffix -*ed*.

Table 1. *Relationships between child and adult grammars*

	!G	G	Learning problems
(i)	*b	a	The substitution problem
(ii)	a,*b	a	The overgeneralization problem
(iii)	a	a,b	The undergeneralization problem
(iv)	a	a	Correct learning
(v)	ϕ	a	The developmental problem

Now take another possibility, already touched upon in connection with the dative alternation, where G has 'a' and !G contains '*b' as well as 'a'; or let us say a rule valid for only 'a' in G is applied to '*b' as well, leading to a more inclusive grammar; see (ii). Both (i) and (ii) indicate that a learner trapped in the predicaments shown in (i) and (ii) is also confronted with an allied difficulty; let us call it *the unlearning problem*: he must somehow find his way back to the correct forms and the only way to do that would be to get rid of incorrect (i) or redundant (ii) forms. Notice that the remedy for (i) could be easier because a rival form exists which would keep turning up in the data and would ultimately be taken into consideration by the learner. Once noticed, furthermore, the learner may not be able to just add it to his grammar as an optional form, creating an overgeneral grammar, because he presumably possesses an appropriate variant of Wexler's Uniqueness Principle (cited in Pinker 1984, Randall 1985; also Osherson et al. 1986a, Wexler and Culicover 1980), which requires that 'in the unmarked case, each verb has one and only one past tense form' (Randall 1985). Not so in the case of (ii) where there is simply a gap in G; the learner is now up against the much more difficult task of taking note of what does not occur at all in the positive evidence.

Still other possibilities are that of undergeneralization, i.e. when G has 'a' and 'b' but !G has only 'a' (iii), and that of perfect correspondence between G and !G (iv). Clearly (iv) does not pose a problem at all; (iii) does, but one with an obvious solution; in fact (iii) is practically unproblematic from a learnability point of view because all that is required is further positive information. Finally, G may have 'a' whereas !G contains nothing comparable to fill the gap (v). This gives rise to another problem, aptly termed *the developmental problem* by Felix (1987) and others; in this case the learner grammar appears to be underspecified for some reason, perhaps having to do with the maturation and growth of the language faculty which is reflected in the intermediate stages of acquisition and causes the progressive restructuring of intermediate grammars to occur; hence the term *maturational hypothesis* which is often employed to refer to this mode of explanation of the problem under consideration.[1] Felix states that 'the principles of Universal Grammar are themselves subject to an innately specified developmental process' (1987: 114); more precisely, he argues that the early child grammar is predominantly built on semantic categories (cf. Gleitman 1981, and see Levy 1983 for a rebuttal), and that it undergoes restructuring largely as a result of the emergence of the X-bar syntax following the onset of the two/three-word stage. The developmental stages in the acquisition of word order in German, on Felix's analysis, should also be explained on similar grounds.[2]

An interesting proposal relying on the maturational hypothesis is developed in Borer and Wexler (1987), who claim that at the early stages child grammars lack the ability to form A-chains, hence verbal passives, which are not possible without A-chain formation that permits an object NP to move to the nonthematic subject position to acquire Case. They cite evidence from both English- and Hebrew-speaking children to support the claim that the passive in child grammars is lexical (i.e. adjectival) rather than verbal.[3] Verbal passivization emerges as soon as movement to an A-position becomes possible. Wexler's (1989) developmental analysis of the control phenomena, and Radford (1988a, 1990) and Platzack's (1990) accounts of the emergence of functional categories in early English and early Swedish, respectively, are along similar lines, as also is Borer and Wexler's (1988) attempt to explain the presence of certain object agreement phenomena in early Italian, which, it is proposed, is constrained by a UG construct termed the Unique External Argument Principle; as this principle ceases to apply in the course of maturation, adult Italian does not evidence these phenomena. (See chapter 5 for a discussion of the implications of the maturational accounts for the development of the null-subject phenomena.)

3.1.6   Unlearning strategies

Setting aside the maturational solution for the time being, let us now consider if some variety of available evidence can help the child overcome some of the learning problems. First we take up the unlearning problem, primarily in relation to the cases where the learner's grammar is overgeneral in the sense of (ii) above (see table 1). As stated before, in such cases positive evidence alone does not seem to be sufficient to cause the retreat to the less general target grammar, since the learner's grammar will always be more inclusive and compatible with the target language. The learner's task, obviously, is not to notice something in the data but to notice the absence thereof, a much more problematic task, especially if the search involved, as in the case of lexical irregularity, is going to be very extensive and complicated (Mazurkewich and White 1984, Randall 1985). If language learners do indeed entertain overgeneral hypotheses, how do they ever manage to retreat to the correct forms without the help of *direct* negative evidence? A number of possibilities have been suggested in the literature (see Pinker 1989: 8ff for an insightful overview), of which the following two, both ultimately dependent on learning by example, are of particular interest here.

(i)   *Indirect negative evidence.*   Chomsky (1981: 8–9) proposes that in certain cases *indirect negative evidence* is available to the learner in the following manner: prior knowledge of the principles of UG makes the learner expect evidence bearing on an unmarked feature of grammar; if such data are not forthcoming, the learner will assume that the language does not possess the unmarked feature and will consequently move on to the corresponding marked one, for which positive evidence would be available (cf. Lasnik 1990, Oehrle 1985; see also Valian 1989, Wexler 1987 1987 for a discussion). For example, take the case of the so-called pro-drop or null-subject parameter. Assuming, as is possible (cf. Rizzi 1980, cited in Berwick 1985: 292), that + pro-drop is the default value for the parameter, the learning of a non-pro-drop language may proceed in this manner. The learner will initially consider + pro-drop, the more inclusive value, to be the correct value. But since examples corroborating this value will not show up in the enumeration of a finite set of data of a certain complexity, the acquisition procedure will instead select the more restrictive (− pro-drop) value. The underlying logic of indirect negative evidence may be represented as below.

(8) ~ P → Q

A very different proposal regarding the use of implicit negative evidence in the fixing of the null-subject parameter is presented in chapter 7.

(ii)   *Indirect positive evidence.*   A related but distinct solution, offered by Randall (1985), is to assume that the learner does not always need *direct*

positive evidence pertaining to a form, that is, evidence which has a one-to-one correspondence with the grammar and which can trigger the acquisition of the relevant grammatical aspect directly. Instead, sometimes positive evidence for one aspect may suffice to *implicationally trigger* the acquisition of another, such an implicational relationship being an outcome of some principle of UG. Randall (1985) presents a solution to the unlearning problem of the dative alternation without recourse to direct or indirect negative information (but see Oehrle 1985 for a proposal relying on implicit negative evidence, and Pinker 1989 for a variety of lexico-semantic possibilities). Her solution is as follows. The dativizable verbs (e.g. *give*) subcategorize for two obligatory objects, whereas those that do not dativize (e.g. *deliver*) subcategorize for only one, the PP (*to*-phrase) in such cases being an optional complement. When the learner wrongly infers a nonalternating verb to be capable of taking two obligatory complements, he soon realizes that he is wrong because the verb in question will occur with a single NP, unlike an alternating verb. If the overgeneral grammar G_1 was like (9), the grammar after the perception of the occurrence of *deliver*-type verbs in a single NP frame, i.e. G_2, would be represented as in (10).

(9) G_1 a. give NP_1 PP   b. deliver NP_1 PP
                    NP NP_1 *NP NP_1
(10) G_2 a. give NP_1 PP   b. deliver NP_1 (PP)
                    NP NP_1 (*NP) NP_1

However, G_2 cannot be maintained on account of a principle of X-bar theory, termed *the Order Principle* (derived from Jackendoff 1977), which states that optional elements must occur outside of the subtree containing obligatorily subcategorized elements. This is illustrated in (11), where H signifies the head that subcategorizes, X the obligatory complement, and Y the optional complement. Here (a) is a grammatical configuration, whereas (b) is not.

(11) a.   *b.

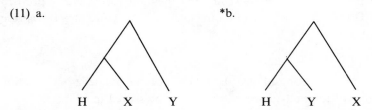

     H   X   Y   H   Y   X

So the learner revises his incorrect subcategorization by expunging the incorrect frame from it, revising G_2 to G_s, the adult steady-state grammar (see 12).

(12) G_s a. give NP_1 PP   b. deliver NP_1 (PP)
      NP NP_1

The outcome of such revision – whether carried out on a verb-by-verb basis, or in terms of semantic subsets of the class of verbs – will obviously be the desired end-state grammar. (The question of course remains as to why the Order Principle is not applied earlier to prevent the overgeneralization in the first place.) To summarize, for the above example the logic of indirect positive evidence goes like this. If a particular verb subcategorizes for a single object and can optionally take a PP, it cannot allow dative alternation because that would involve movement of the optional element to an illegitimate position between the subcategorizing head V and the obligatory complement NP. Formally:

(13) $P \rightarrow \sim Q$

Putting aside direct negative evidence, it should follow that only *direct* positive evidence bears a one-to-one relationship with the parts of grammar acquired. By definition, both the remaining types of evidence (which might as well be considered to be subtypes of appropriate learning strategies) have merely an indirect relationship with the grammar, the process of fixation of the correct generalization being partly deductive, in comparison with the more inductive type of learning resulting from direct positive evidence.[4]

3.1.7 Instantaneous versus incremental learning

Now we return to the developmental problem and some related issues. According to a standard simplifying assumption language acquisition is considered to be instantaneous (Chomsky 1965, 1986a), a legitimate idealization as far as linguistic theory is concerned. Under this assumption all the data are supposed to be accessible to the child at once, and his task is considered to be that of applying an evaluation metric and choosing the highest valued grammar (from among the possible ones) which is compatible with the data. As far as the actual course of acquisition is concerned, it is evident that the process is not instantaneous, but noninstantaneous (Berwick 1985), occurring in stages as formally sketched below, where the relationship of evidence and grammar is (still) considerably idealized.

  We represent the learning procedure as a function f, and the data successively available to the learner as $D_1, D_2, \ldots$. The initial state of a grammar (determined by UG) is written as G_o, various intermediate grammars as G_i for all i ($0 \leqslant i \leqslant s-1$), and a final steady-state grammar as G_s. Starting off with a nonempty initial state G_o (constrained by UG), the learner is presented with an ever expanding amount of language data, from which he infers a series of intermediate grammars ($G_1, G_2, \ldots$) (also see figure 1).

(14) G_o
$f(G_o,D_1)=G_1$
$f(G_1,D_2)=G_2$
$f(G_2,D_3)=G_3$
$\vdots$
$f(G_i,D_{i+1})=G_{i+1}$
         (where $0 \leqslant i \leqslant s-1$)
G_s

Each new intermediate grammar is selected on the basis of the previous grammar as well as the new datum; any previous data do not play any role in the process, which means the learner is not obliged to remember any amount of past data. In other words the process is *intensional*. Previous conjectures (i.e. G_i) and the current datum (D_{i+1}) are mapped by the learning function f to a new grammar G_{i+1}; so, if necessary, the output of every step is modified as a result of the new datum, and thus becomes the input for the next step. This process continues till eventually G_s, the steady-state grammar of the ambient language, is attained.

Given the foregoing incremental model of language acquisition, a fundamental issue regarding the development of grammar is the epistemological status of learner grammars. Do these grammars really exist as such

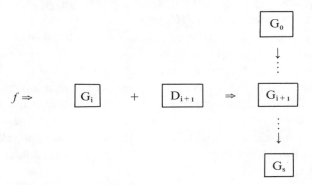

Figure 1: Incremental learning

in the mind, or are they, at least in part, mere artefacts of certain performance constraints? To what extent are the universal principles of language applicable to such grammars? Why do children, distinctly and uniformly, pass through different developmental stages while learning language; in other words, what is the explanation for the developmental problem and the related incremental course of language acquisition? With respect to this question at least two positions can be taken, which we shall briefly describe here.

The first proposal constitutes, to borrow Chomsky's (1987a) terminology, a 'no-growth' theory of language acquisition. Pinker (1984) proposes that the null hypothesis should be that child grammars are built on exactly the same principles as adult ones; this *continuity hypothesis* (comparable to Randall's 1985 Formal Parallels Hypothesis) requires that the differences between child and adult grammars be explained in terms of common or parallel linguistic principles. Hyams (1985), likewise, claims that 'linguistic theory is also a theory of actual grammatical development – perhaps the only acquisition theory that is necessary'; more concretely, Hyams (1986) states that 'given the range of variation defined by each parameter', it is possible 'that the early grammar of a language L may differ from the adult grammar of L with respect to the value specified for a particular parameter, provided that the value chosen falls within the permitted range' (ibid.: 5). A major consequence of the foregoing claims is that child grammars are possible adult grammars.

According to the continuity hypothesis the initial linguistic state the child starts off with is fixed, and is governed by the same universal principles as those underlying adult grammar. Insofar as child language is adequately describable on the basis of tenets of linguistic theory, the hypothesis holds; differences between the child grammar(s) and the adult grammar of a particular language, and the restructuring that is witnessed in language development, can be demonstrated to occur within the range of variation fixed by linguistic theory (see Hyams 1986, discussed in detail in chapters 4 and 5, for a demonstration of this kind of analysis). However, a problem arises as soon as we turn to differences of a nature not explicable within the permitted range of linguistic variation, particularly when child grammars, as in very early stages, appear to be not just different but clearly lacking certain basic categories or properties. A further problem associated with this line of reasoning, given the assumption that child grammars are compatible with adult ones, is to explain why restructuring occurs in the first place, and moreover why it occurs when it does occur.

One possible explanation, necessary to account for the developmental problem under the continuity hypothesis, is that child grammars are grammars of perceived data only, that is, of parts of the data which the learner is able to analyse at any particular stage in language development (White 1981, 1982). Presumably the child's perception of data increases as the perceptual system grows and acquires greater processing and retention capacity, prompting reorganization in the child's grammar. This assumption is problematic in many respects. As Felix puts it, 'According to White [1982] the temporal aspect of language development has nothing to do with principles of Universal Grammar, parameter-fixing and the like, but is strictly a matter of perception. It is only *after* perception has changed that Universal Grammar comes into play' (1987: 111). Felix further argues that White's solution (an essential consequence of the continuity hypothesis) is incomplete in the absence of a principled theory of perceptual change; it only removes the problem from the domain of linguistic inquiry and vaguely relocates it within a theory of perception, ignoring the equally compelling possibility that the child's 'grammatical knowledge determines this linguistic perception, rather than the other way round' (ibid.: 112). On pain of circularity one could say that developmental change occurs as much because the perception of a new datum is made possible by the current grammar as due to the perception of a new datum which renders a revision in the grammar necessary. (Also see Borer and Wexler 1987 on these issues.)

An alternative solution to the developmental problem, already touched upon, constitutes a 'growth' theory (Chomsky 1987a), which assumes that the initial linguistic state is underspecified, does not remain fixed, and matures with the passage of time, thus acquiring greater complexity. This approach is compatible with a view incorporating concomitant perceptual development, but does not depend on it in any crucial way as far as language acquisition is concerned. Further, in general it does not assume any qualitative discontinuity between child and adult grammars; the two types of grammar are assumed to be similar, but not coextensive. Some versions of this view, e.g. Felix (1987), however, do allow child grammars, which, strictly speaking, are not possible adult grammars (see note 2 below).

To briefly evaluate the first two proposals, it seems that the 'no-growth' theory cannot adequately explain the developmental facts of acquisition, although the assumptions underlying it might well be highly desirable from the viewpoint of methodological consistency and simplicity. The 'growth' theory, on the other hand, imposes the additional burden of (ultimately) explaining the stages of development, but could possibly be closer to empirical facts. After all growth of some kind is attested in the case of most biological organs, and if the faculty underlying language is a biological entity, then there is no necessary reason why it should come into existence fully grown and not undergo the process of ontogenetic change typical of other biological systems. The 'growth' view, moreover, combines the advantages of theoretical consistency with those of developmental flexibility. It is, therefore, possible that, in order for linguistic theory to be meaningfully related to child language development, a theory of successive emergence of linguistic entities is necessary; it would, of course, be highly desirable for such a theory to be able to explain why and in what manner a grammar G_n acquires characteristics lacking in the preceding developmental grammar G_{n-1}.

3.2   Formal models and their linguistic relevance

In the following pages we present a brief survey of some formal models of language learning, in particular the 'identification in the limit' model (Gold 1967), the degree-2 theory (Wexler and Culicover 1980), and the generalized identification model (Osherson et al. 1984).[5] Our purpose in reviewing these models is to demonstrate their rigorous method of probing issues and their relevance to the linguistic and psychological study of language acquisition.

3.2.1   Identification in the limit

Mathematical models based on the theory of inductive inference originate with Gold (1967). The influential Gold study offers a pioneering model often called 'identification in the limit'. Gold's conclusions apply to entire classes of formal languages, based on those included in the Chomsky hierarchy (Chomsky and Miller 1963).

To assist the reader's memory, at this point we shall deviate a little to provide a thumb-nail sketch of the languages in the hierarchy.[6] Every *recursively enumerable* language can be generated by a grammar, which will output or enumerate all the sentences in the language, but no decision procedure for distinguishing nonsentences exists for some languages in the class. A class of languages is *recursive* if there is a decision procedure for every input sentence, whether or not the input sentence is in a language, but there is no effective way of knowing whether such a language is decidable. In the case of *primitive recursive* languages, the decidability of each language is known. The classes defined so far are relatively unrestricted insofar as the permissible form of production rules underlying them is concerned. In contrast, the further three classes in the hierarchy originate from increasingly restrictive conditions on the form of the rules of their respective classes of grammars. Thus *context-sensitive* languages have grammars that allow specification of the context in which a nonterminal symbol can be rewritten as a (non-null) string of symbols; in contrast, *context-free* grammars allow such replacement of symbols regardless of the context in which the symbol to be rewritten appears. *Regular* grammars permit a nonterminal symbol to be rewritten as a string of terminal symbols followed or preceded by at most a single nonterminal symbol. Finally, *finite cardinality* languages consist of only a finite number of sentences, and their grammars need not contain any nonterminal symbols. (Each class is associated with a particular type of abstract automaton, tokens of which can generate the sentences of its members.)

More significantly for our purposes, every finite cardinality language is also a regular language; every regular language is also a context-free language; every context-free language is also a context-sensitive language; and likewise with respect to the languages higher in the hierarchy. But the converse is not true. In other words, these classes of languages are differentiated on the basis of the type of rules contained in grammars that generate them, and each class in the hierarchy properly contains the classes below it (table 2).

The Gold paradigm took into account classes of possible languages (as set out in table 2), a criterion of successful acquisition (or identifiability), a method of information presentation, and finally a learning procedure which converted data into hypotheses. (In Gold's formulation languages are not distinct from grammatical hypotheses entertained by the learner.) Time was quantized and at each step the learner was presented with a unit of information and asked to guess the identity of the unknown language. A class of languages was said to be identifiable in the limit if after observation of a sequence of data from any language in the class, the learner came to hypothesize the language in some finite time, and thereafter maintained this hypothesis. The learner identified the correct language by enumerating all the possible hypotheses until he hit the one which was compatible with the data observed to date.[7] Note that the identifiability criterion did not require

Table 2. *Classes of languages and their learnability*

Class	Learnable from:	
	Informant presentation	Text presentation
Recursively enumerable	−	−
Decidable recursive	−	−
Primitive recursive	+	−
Context-sensitive	+	−
Context-free	+	−
Regular (finite state)	+	−
Finite cardinality	+	+

the learner to stop and be aware of the fact that he had succeeded; he could go on observing and guessing forever.

Access to data could take the form of either *text presentation* or *informant presentation*. A text was defined as an arbitrary enumeration of positive sentences such that every string in the language appeared at least once. Informant presentation, in contrast, additionally allowed the learner negative feedback from an informant, who specified whether or not a sentence was in the language to be learned each time an input datum was made available. Gold's major result was to show that only the most trivial class of languages, i.e. finite cardinality languages, was learnable from positive evidence alone (i.e. text presentation), and that the classes up to the primitive recursive one became identifiable only if negative (or informant) presentation was allowed.

Gold's learnability results are significantly negative, in view of the fact that (direct) negative information is generally held not to be available to the child learner, not systematically and exhaustively anyway. However, for a number of reasons they cannot be relevant to the acquisition of language by children.

(i) They are true only of the classes of formal languages investigated by Gold, none of which is known to be coextensive with the class of natural languages. It is certain that natural languages are constrained 'from the bottom', and are neither finite cardinality nor finite state. It is almost certain that they are not context-free either (Higginbotham 1984, Shieber 1985). Beyond that very little is definite. Attempts have been made to identify learnability with recursiveness, recursiveness serving as the upper bound on the formal complexity of languages. However, it has been persuasively argued (e.g. Chomsky 1980, ch. 3, Lasnik 1981, Matthews 1979) that natural languages may not be recursive, or even recursively enumerable (Langendoen and Postal 1984). Chomsky points out that questions of generative capacity are not empirically significant in the least:

> The richness of the class of languages admitted by UG (its generative capacity) is a matter of no obvious empirical import. What is important is a requirement of 'feasibility' that has no clear relation to scope of UG. What is required for feasibility is that given data, only a fairly small collection of languages be made available for inspection or evaluation (e.g. languages might be sufficiently 'scattered' in value so that only few are so available). A theory of UG might fail to satisfy the feasibility requirement if its scope were finite and might satisfy it if it were to permit the maximum variety of rule systems in a sense that can be made precise. Other facts concerning the structure of UG are relevant at this point, not generative capacity. (1986a: 55)

Since the significant questions have to do with matters of empirical fact, not those of generative capacity (also see Chomsky 1965: 60–2, Berwick and Weinberg 1984),[8] Gold's mathematical results may not have any direct bearing on the issues of natural language acquisition.

(ii) Gold's characterization of languages is empirically insufficient for still another reason. Gold (1967) himself points out that in his learnability model 'a very naive model of language is assumed', as language is defined extensionally as a set of strings on some finite alphabet. On the other hand natural languages, as is well known, are intricately structured and are not at all mere sets of strings.

(iii) Gold's learning procedure is psychologically deficient because it demands excessive processing capacity. The enumeration procedure adopted by Gold, though useful because it is maximally powerful, can take astronomically large amounts of time in the identification of a language. In Pinker's words:

> The learner's predicament is reminiscent of Jorge Luis Borges's 'librarian of Babel', who searches a vast library containing books with all possible combinations of alphabetic characters for the book that clarifies the basic mysteries of humanity. (1979: 227–8)

'Identification in the limit' clearly is not a good enough criterion for natural language learning; something like 'identification in the *natural* limit' most probably would be! This, however, does not invalidate the negative learnability results obtained by Gold in connection with the languages in the Chomsky hierarchy. Since no procedure more powerful than enumeration exists, the learner as characterized by Gold is not hampered by any cognitive constraints. Therefore anything that is not learnable for him will remain unlearnable for any other less powerful learning procedure.

Overall, the Gold model was successful in demonstrating that mathematical investigation of the learnability of even relatively trivial classes of languages can yield some interesting results. In particular, he showed that in a learning theory any variation in the nature of input, e.g. that embodied in the contrast between positive and negative information, has very different learnability implications.

The line of inquiry started by Gold has since progressed in two distinct directions. One group of researchers, led by Kenneth Wexler, has tried to study learnability of languages characterized by transformational grammars. The other group, led by Daniel Osherson, has sought to generalize the concept of identification in many logically possible ways, though in their work natural languages continue to be specified extensionally, i.e. as consisting of sets of strings. Both types of inquiry are briefly reviewed in the following sections.

3.2.2   Degree-2 learnability and its extensions

More linguistically inspired learnability models are also concerned with the formal aspects of language learning, but in a manner much more constrained by some theoretically significant theory of natural language. Thus Wexler and Culicover (1980) and Morgan (1986) are grounded in the Standard Theory transformational grammar, and Pinker (1982) in Lexical–Functional Grammar or LFG (Bresnan 1982). Here we are largely interested in Wexler and Culicover's degree-2 learnability theory (Wexler and Culicover 1980, also Wexler 1981, 1982; see Osherson et al. 1986b for a formal analysis of the learning paradigm underlying the theory).

The degree-2 theory directly addresses the issue of the learnability of transformational grammars. The key requirement is that the positive evidence necessary for the learning of the language to be learned should be available through relatively simple sentences; to be precise, through sentences of complexity of degree-2 or less (hence the name of the theory), where degree-2 denotes the degree of embedding of the cyclic node S in a phrase marker. The forms of phrase markers of degree-0, -1 and -2 are illustrated below.

(15) a. Degree-0

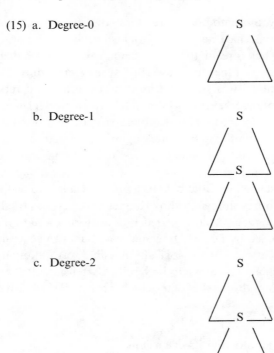

b. Degree-1

c. Degree-2

The theory is a triplet, consisting of the following components (Wexler 1982).

(16)a. A class of possible grammars *G*
   b. Input, *I*, about a member of *G*
   c. A learning procedure *P* which infers a grammar in *G* on the basis of relevant *I*

The learning procedure is required to learn according to a criterion *C*, which is that at each time t_i in the infinite sequence of data for any arbitrarily chosen grammar in *G*, *P* should be able to select a grammar each time until at some finite time the target grammar is selected, following which the learner does not alter his guess. (Actually the criterion of success is probabilistic.) Unlike Gold, the class of languages studied is an empirically plausible one: i.e. the class of transformational grammars

(Chomsky 1965). Input is supposed to consist of (b,s) pairs, that is pairs of base phrase markers (or deep structures) and unique surface structures derived from them. The learner's task is to learn the transformational component from such data, as the base component is held to be largely predetermined. The access to deep structures is hypothesized to be made possible by means of semantic information.

The method of proof is the demonstration that whenever the learner makes an error, it is detectable on a phrase marker of degree-2 or less. A learnability result for the class of grammars in question was obtained by Wexler and Culicover by introducing certain constraints on the operation of transformations. Some of these constraints are: (i) *the binary principle* (comparable to subjacency; see chapter 2), which states that 'a transformation may apply to the level at which it is operating, plus the next lower level, but no further down' (Wexler and Culicover 1980: 109), i.e. only within subtrees dominated by two adjacent cyclic nodes; (ii) *the freezing principle*, which requires that 'if a transformation changes the structure of a node so that it is no longer a base structure, nothing under that node may be analysed (and thus changed) by a further transformation' (Wexler and Culicover 1980: 119), since now that node is *frozen*; (iii) *the raising principle*, which says that if a node is raised, then no further transformations can apply to any nodes dominated by the raised node; in the words of Wexler and Culicover, 'If a node A is raised, then no node that A dominates may be used to fit a transformation' (1980: 143).

Wexler and Culicover's degree-2 learnability result is an achievement in that it is *relatively* feasible (in the sense of Chomsky 1965). Recall that Chomsky proposes a number of criteria of empirical adequacy required of linguistic theory. The familiar ones are those related to the 'question of adequacy-in-principle' (1965: 54), i.e. *descriptive adequacy* and *explanatory adequacy*. An even stronger criterion is that of *feasibility*, which requires that a given acquisition procedure should 'succeed in producing grammars within the given constraints of time and access, and within the range of observed uniformity of output' (ibid.: 54) (cf. the quotation above from Chomsky 1986a). This is comparable to Wexler and Culicover's view: they explain that 'feasibility may be called "easy learnability"', that is, learnability from fairly restricted primary data, in a sufficiently quick time, with limited use of memory' (1980: 19).

Thus the degree-2 framework uses an empirically plausible model of syntax as the basis for the class of learnable grammars, and does not demand either negative data of any sort or data of a very complex nature.

The learner is not supposed to be confronted with all the data at once, nor does he have to enumerate all the possible grammars one by one, each in its entirety, and subject them to an evaluation metric. Instead the process of data observation is gradual, and grammars are learned incrementally on a rule-by-rule basis; the learner can either add a new rule to the grammar, or delete one in a single step, but he is not permitted to change a rule. (This is somewhat comparable to the fixing of parameters one after another; see the next chapter.) Learning decisions are made on the basis of the current grammar and the current datum and no memory for the past data is required; in other words, the learning procedure is *intensional*. In short, the learning system is not psychologically unfettered, like that of Gold, nor overly idealized, as the instantaneity assumption of Chomsky (1965) is relaxed.

In spite of its tremendous achievements there are problems with the model, not surprisingly as the task it accomplished was extensive enough as it was, and perhaps it was good that it did not try to do more. A major overall problem is that linguistic theory has changed rapidly, having evolved into a highly restrictive system of representations and principles (see chapter 2) which is arguably no longer in need of the kind of mathematical treatment the Standard Theory was capable of invoking. As Chomsky remarks:

The conclusion that only a finite number of core grammars are available in principle has consequences for the mathematical investigation of generative power and of learnability. In certain respects, the conclusion trivializes these investigations. (1981: 11)

The degree-2 theory, therefore, may not have much substantive relevance to the issues currently being investigated. Nevertheless, it has made a significant contribution to the evolution of argumentation in the theory of learnability. For example, it has demonstrated that the degree of data required could be a crucial variable in determining the learnability of any class of grammars. As a result the complexity of data is likely to remain an important consideration in most accounts of learnability. Thus Morgan (1986) delineates a degree-1 proof, which modifies the framework of Wexler and Culicover by introducing *the Bracketed Input Hypothesis*. This results in enriching the concept of input considerably, and in somewhat reducing the role of the innate endowment of the child. To be precise, Morgan claims that input is *bracketed*: it contains cues indicating the way the words group into syntactic constituents and subconstituents (cf. Morgan, Meier and Newport 1988). The significant learnability result which follows is that Standard Theory transformational grammars are learnable on the basis of data with degree of embedding equal to or less than one (see 15b).

Likewise, Culicover and Wilkins (1984) attempt an informal learnability sketch which exploits some of the insights gained from the degree-2 theory. The sketch takes into consideration the learnability of the class of grammars specified by a version of generative theory developed in the greater part of the same work. The notable characteristic of the theory is that the concept of locality enters into all of its major components, one important consequence of which is that grammars characterized by such a theory may possibly be learnable from degree-0 data only (see 15a). Largely formulated in linguistic terms, Lightfoot (1989) delineates a comparable informal degree-0 analysis, also assuming locality but executed strictly within the principles-and-parameters approach. He asserts that since, arguably, most syntactic operations can be defined over projections of degree-0 or at most those slightly beyond the degree-0 range, the subset of evidence crucially required by the child in order to trigger the correct generalizations need not contain examples of complexity greater than that specified above.[9]

3.2.3   Identification generalized

In a series of publications Osherson and his colleagues have attempted to generalize and improve Gold's identification model in several possible ways (see Osherson et al. 1986a, and the references cited therein).[10] As in Gold, the learner is construed as a function that maps environments into grammars. (Actually both evidence and grammars are coded as natural numbers, and the learning function is any function from numbers representing finite sequences of evidence into numbers coding grammars that are successively represented in the learner's mind.)

The identification model is generalized along three dimensions: the environment for learning, the criterion for successful learning, and the learning strategy. Variations in these components of the language learning process are introduced on empirical grounds and their consequences mathematically worked out. For example, environments are allowed to be noisy or incomplete, i.e. they can have a finite amount of intrusion of nonsentences, or they may systematically omit certain data. Interestingly, it can be mathematically shown that thus expanding the type of environment reduces the capacity of the learning functions to identify certain languages. Similarly, the criterion of success is relaxed to permit the identification, in some finite time, of an approximation of the ambient language, and the learner is not required to continue to stick to the same approximate language for all further times. It seems that various combinations of criteria of correctness and stabilization yield different identifiability results. The nature of the learning strategies is also altered to bring it closer to human learning. For instance, the learning function is not just considered to be computable; it is further restricted to be nontrivial, i.e. to be able to select only grammars which generate infinite languages, clearly under the assumption that natural languages are infinite collections of sentences.

To illustrate further, Osherson et al. (1984) make some alternative assumptions about certain components of the learning paradigm, such as the following: the learning function is computable, nontrivial, and conservative; also, alternative characterizations of environments and identification are employed. This leads to the formulation of an interesting thesis about natural language, which is called Strong Nativism. Strong nativism means that 'no more than finitely many natural languages differ infinitely from each other' (Osherson et al. 1984: 20); in the words of Chomsky 'there are only finitely many *essentially different* languages' (1986a: 149). In spite of the fact that the assumptions regarding the nature of language in Osherson et al. (1984) are minimal, e.g. languages are characterized as sets of strings, and their generalized identification model is at most concerned with the weak equivalence of the grammatical systems learned,[11] or with E-languages (see Chomsky 1986a: 149–50, also 213–14n), the finiteness hypothesis offered by Osherson et al. appears to be in accord with Chomsky's more empirically motivated assertion that the number of core languages, as characterized by the principles and parameters of UG, is finite. This is interesting, since Chomsky's claim springs entirely from linguistic reasons, suggesting that at least some aspects of Osherson et al.'s approach are empirically well-founded. We would like to stress that even though formal learning-theoretic investigation along the lines adumbrated above leads to insights of considerable significance, they stand or fall by the empirical validity of the underlying assumptions. As Osherson et al. remark, 'It cannot be emphasized too strongly that in the absence of empirically motivated hypotheses about language acquisition, Learning Theory is an empty formalism, of little relevance to natural language' (1984: 24).

3.2.4   Methodological implications

The development of the mathematical theory of learnability is instructive in several ways for the relatively informal type of linguistic learnability research, as for instance attempted in the present study. We have briefly shown that formal investigation of natural language learning has increasingly come to adopt assumptions which are more relevant to the empirical conditions of that type of learning. The impetus for the shift has often come from linguistic theory or from the study of child language acquisition. The important question to consider is whether there are still some generally held assumptions which need to be modified for substantial reasons. Linguistically oriented learnability research can play a major role by raising and perhaps (hopefully) answering such questions, with obvious repercussions in the field of formal learnability. In return, the linguistic approaches can learn a great deal from the mathematical ones, particularly with respect to the need for rigour and precision in the formulation of relevant concepts, though not necessarily involving formalization. As Chomsky remarks:

In atomic theory, or genetics, or other branches of the natural sciences, a particular version of a theory may be made precise, with a particular presentation (formalization) characterizing its objects and an axiom system generating theorems. In practice, the natural sciences do not bother very much with formalization, except in specific subparts of a theory where it is important for proving theorems or drawing out the consequences of assumptions when it is difficult to do so without a precise formulation. Formalization itself is not a very difficult task, but it is generally premature and pointless: in fact, until rather recently in the history of mathematics, even the concept of formalization, or proof, was not understood in our sense, and furthermore, mathematicians had few qualms in using concepts that were extremely unclear and perhaps made little sense ... The concepts of formalization were developed in mathematics when they were useful or necessary to carry mathematical research further; apart from that, it is a pointless exercise. There was a time, some few years ago, when it was considered a worthwhile endeavour to carry out formalization in the natural sciences ... but there are few illusions now on these matters, outside of such fields as linguistics. Here, as always, precise formulation is in order to the extent that it facilitates proving theorems or determining the consequences of assumptions; it is important to express one's ideas with as much precision as is required, say, in formulating binding theory or the Empty Category Principle. But true formalization is rarely a useful device in linguistics, which does not have the intellectual depth that might require this exercise. Those who think otherwise have the task of showing what results can be achieved by steps in this direction. (1987b: 13)

At any rate, ideally the two research paradigms should operate parallel to each other, to the extent of using comparable theoretical constructs, so that the exchange of information can take place on a regular and systematic basis (see the papers in Manaster-Ramer 1987 for a recent review of the empirical significance of the mathematical analysis of language). This would be highly desirable since, although the methodologies and tools employed are different, the ultimate goals are held in common between the two approaches.

3.3   Summary

In this chapter we have surveyed different components formulating a possible learning theory for language. The notion of a learning paradigm was introduced to emphasize the significance of precise definitions of factors implicated in the learning theory for the domain of language. The different learning problems related to the different types of evidence were analysed at some length. Since the knowledge of the language-specific facts is undoubtedly determined by environment, we have tried to outline various relations between environments and the knowledge of grammars acquired. The following four different modes of the presentation and use of evidence were considered.

(17)a. Direct positive evidence
   b. Indirect positive evidence
   c. Indirect negative evidence
   d. Direct negative evidence

It was pointed out that whereas (17d) is not relevant to natural language learning, (17a–c) might be involved in the process to varying degrees, perhaps together forming the input data for natural language acquisition, with the use of (17a) being inherent in the core mechanisms of the domain-specific learning.

   Certain fundamental concepts and results from formal learning theory were also discussed. It seems that at a broader conceptual level the progress in the theory has proceeded parallel with the developments in linguistic theory, indicating a gradual shift towards assumptions which are empirically constrained to a greater extent. However, it should be obvious that at the empirical level formal learning-theoretic investigations are out of step with linguistic theory, which has come to rely more and more on concepts and methods that are intrinsically germane to the study of natural language. An intriguing prospect for the future is a bridging of the gap between the two research paradigms. Hence, in the next chapter we proceed to an exploration of the parameter-setting model in the light of the basic concepts deployed in this and the previous two chapters.

4 Approaches to parameter fixation

This chapter begins to explore some central learnability and acquisitional issues with reference to the parameter-setting model of language learnability. Two broad approaches, namely the formal approach and the developmental approach, are considered. First a formal overview of the model is presented; this is followed by the description of a specific formal proposal, namely the set-theoretical approach to parameter fixation presented in Wexler and Manzini (1987) and Manzini and Wexler (1987). Then a developmental interpretation of the model, largely based on Hyams (1986), is described at some length.

4.1 The formal approach

Let us start with a general outline of the essential background to this approach, briefly recapitulating some material from the previous chapter. The *Aspects* model (Chomsky 1965) viewed linguistic competence as a product of the ability of a hypothetical language acquisition device (or LAD) to construct transformational grammars after having operated on a set of primary linguistic data. Linguistic theory so conceived provided an enumeration of possible grammars G_1, G_2, ..., G_n, and an evaluation measure that would assign values to the potential grammars. Acquisition (in an abstract and idealized sense) occurred as a result of the selection of the most highly valued grammar which was compatible with the data. The LAD was construed as a system of formulation and evaluation of hypotheses, the latter being grammars each of which had to be selected or rejected *in toto*. Wexler and Culicover (1980), while recognizing the value of the instantaneous approach for the purposes of linguistic theory, sought to develop a more incremental, noninstantaneous framework which permitted modification of grammars by the addition or deletion (but not change) of individual rules. By comparison, parameter fixation is not a process of either selection or modification of whole grammars; it consists of the independent selection of preexisting parameter values whose interaction is hypothesized to yield the grammar of a language.

4.1.1   The model

The learner's initial state is supposed to consist of a set of universal principles which specify some limited possibilities of variation, expressible in terms of parameters which need to be fixed in one of the few possible ways. The fixing of the parameters of UG, combined with the learning of an appropriate lexicon, yields the knowledge of a language. A parameter is associated with a limited number of values, constituting the search space for it, and the learner's task, given relevant evidence, is that of search through this space, the aim being to infer the identity of the correct value from among the permissible ones. One may accordingly characterize parameter setting as bounded search for the identification of the correct parameter values underlying the language to be learned. A parameter is said to be fixed if it is assigned a value consistent with the observed primary evidence; a value is consistent with the evidence just in case it matches every relevant (positive) instance presented to the learner. Relevant instances are those which exhibit the structural configurations and other properties that the parameter addresses. Thus parameter setting, idealized to the fixing of a single parameter, requires at least the following if it is to occur as noted.

(1)a. a parameter p with n ($n > 1$) values, and a specification of the structural configurations in which p can take a value.
   b. an ambient language $L(p_i)$ which is associated with value p_i of p, for all i ($1 \leqslant i \leqslant n$).
   c. a set of (positive) examples E matching the structural configurations relevant to p.
   d. a learning principle that, given E, identifies the correct value of p for L (p_i).

Clearly, an example δ leads to the identification of a value p_i of parameter p if the learner is capable, in the first place, of representing δ as relevent to p_i.

Ideally the learner is presented with positive data pertaining to the target language one by one. Each datum is processed and interpreted by him to the extent that his (cognitive/linguistic) capacities allow him. If sufficiently interpretable, the datum prompts the learner to make a guess as to the value of some parameter. The learner stays with this guess until the environment offers or the learner is able to perceive a sentence which is in the ambient language but not in the learner's language as it was formerly conjectured. This makes the learner change his mind and adopt the next parameter value which is compatible with the data. This process continues till in some finite time the learner's language, as reflected in the parameter value, is consistent with the ambient language.

It should be stressed that parameter setting cannot explain all aspects of language acquisition. As Williams points out, 'It would be quite surprising if parameter setting exhausted the possibilities – knowledge of language involves a number of different types of knowledge, and acquisition will proceed most efficiently if the means of learning each type is tailored to that type' (1987: xii). Lexical forms and their relationship with corresponding meanings, for instance, cannot be said to follow from parameter setting in any significant way. Williams further points out that even when parameter setting does seem an apt description of what occurs, it assumes previous knowledge of things which are to be parameterized. Above, this presupposed knowledge is implied to enter into the structural configurations over which a parameter is defined. It could be a product of the previous fixation of a number of parameters, or it could be a result of some kind of 'pre-parametric learning'. In any case, 'clearly, some limited amount of the language must be learned before the questions about how to set parameters can be raised' (Williams 1987: xvii). We therefore maintain that all the parameters belonging to a language are not set simultaneously – instantaneously, as it were (Chomsky 1965, 1986a) – but that some may be set earlier than others and some later, either because a parameter cannot be set until some others have been fixed, or because a specific maturational schedule is in operation. Note that a noninstantaneous view entails a temporal sequence, thought one which may not necessarily correspond to the developmental stages of acquisition (Berwick 1985), as, for instance, maintained by Hyams (1986).

Considering that the language learner's task is merely to examine a prescribed choice space to identify a parameter value, it might appear that the learnability problems posed by the parameter-setting model would be rather trivial (cf. Chomsky 1981: 11). However, substantial problems emerge in a learnability treatment of parameter setting. Even in a highly restricted search space convergence on the correct value can be problematic without some sort of pattern dictating the search. For example, as illustrated below, the order in which the values of a given parameter are considered by the child could be important at least in the case of some parameters. So it might be important to discover an evaluation metric whereby the set of values of a parameter could be ordered.

One obvious possibility is that the ordering of the values of a parameter is to be derived from markedness, the latter being entirely justifiable on linguistic-theoretic grounds. On this view markedness will be treated as a given fact which a learnability theorist may have to take into account; of course it is conceivable that this type of markedness could well be altogether irrelevant to learnability-theoretic concerns. Conversely, it is also possible that markedness is fundamentally a function of learning factors, in which case it could in some way be reflected in the evidence available to the child learner. The question then arises: do the languages generated by the values of the same parameter differ from each other such that the learner's choice can be smoothly directed by examples characteristic of them?

Let us suppose, for the purpose of illustration, that there is a parameter p with two values p_i and p_j, and that the languages resulting from the adoption of the respective values are $L(p_i)$ and $L(p_j)$.[1] Since p_i and p_j represent the loci of variation along the *same* parameter p, it would be pertinent to ask how different $L(p_i)$ and $L(p_j)$ are from each other. For example, $L(p_i)$ may or may not share some sentences with $L(p_j)$, or it could be a larger or a smaller language than $L(p_j)$. In set-theoretical terms, the possible ways in which the two languages could be so related are set out below (also see figure 2).

(2)a. $L(p_i) \subseteq L(p_j)$ or $L(p_j) \subseteq L(p_i)$; i.e. either $L(p_i)$ is a subset of $L(p_j)$, or $L(p_i)$ is a subset of $L(p_i)$.
   b. $L(p_i) \cap L(p_j) \neq \emptyset$, such that neither of the languages is a subset of the other; i.e. $L(p_i)$ and $L(p_j)$ partially intersect (henceforth all references to intersection will be in this restricted sense, also schematized in figure 2, b).
   c. $L(p_i) \cap L(p_j) = \emptyset$: i.e. $L(p_i)$ and $L(p_j)$ are disjoint.

In the case of both (2b) and (2c) learning should proceed smoothly, as wrong conjectures can be rectified very easily from positive data, no matter which value is selected first. With respect to intersecting languages as described in (2b), there will always be at least one datum which is in $L(p_i)$ but not in $L(p_j)$, or at least one datum which is in $L(p_j)$ but not in $L(p_i)$, which will bring about the desired change in the learner's grammar. As far as (2c) is concerned, since $L(p_i)$ and $L(p_j)$ are totally disjoint, the choices will be made independently in a straightforward fashion, with no possibility of error. To sum up, the values of a parameter yielding intersecting and disjoint sets may be considered to be unordered from a purely learning-theoretic perspective (presumably, linguistic considerations may nonetheless require some other type of markedness).

Now assume that some parameters of UG have values which are related

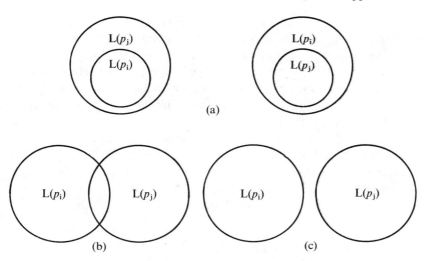

Figure 2: Relations between languages

in the manner of (2a); specifically, suppose that $L(p_i) \subseteq L(p_j)$. If the values of one such parameter were unordered with respect to precedence of choice, and consequently p_j, the more inclusive value, could be selected on the basis of data from $L(p_i)$, then the learner might have to face what Manzini and Wexler call the 'subset problem' (1987:414), a particularization of the familiar overgeneralization problem.[2] Consider that the correct value was p_i. Then the learner would be in the potential danger of guessing the superset language first, in which case positive-only evidence would not help. In the absence of any kind of negative information, the learner could find himself in a situation where recovering p_i, the correct (less inclusive) value would be logically impossible since every instance of $L(p_i)$ would also be in $L(p_j)$, the incorrectly conjectured language, and therefore no positive data would be able to disconfirm the wrong conjecture. As Gold pointed out, 'The problem with text [i.e. positive data] is that, if you guess too large a language, the text will never tell you that you are wrong' (1967: 461).

However, notice that the learner will not face any problem in selecting one of the two values provided the less inclusive value, namely the one generating the subset language, has to be chosen first. More concretely, suppose, as before, that p_i happens to be the less inclusive value. Then on the basis of (direct) positive evidence the learner will be able to identify either of the two values, depending on which is the correct one. He might correctly select one or the other value straightaway, or alternatively, in the event of p_j being the correct choice, might entertain p_i as an intermediate choice for a while before ultimately proceeding to p_j, partly in keeping with Hyams's (1986) developmental view of parameter setting. In any event, he will be in no danger of being stuck with the superset language; the overgeneralization problem will not arise in the first place, since the learning system is conservatively constrained so that, given evidence compatible with both the languages but not containing any examples which only belong to $L(p_j)$, it cannot select the larger language without first considering the smaller one. (Cf. Baker 1979, Dell 1981.) Wexler and Manzini present exactly such a conservative proposal to avoid the subset problem, aptly named (following Berwick 1985, 1886) *the subset principle*.

4.1.2   Binding theory and the subset principle

The subset principle had been foreshadowed in Baker (1979) and Dell's (1981) proposals, and in Williams's (1981a) principle of minimal falsifiability, before it was given its present name by Berwick (1985).[3] Formally, the historical antecedents of the principle can be traced back to Gold's (1967) seminal study of the hierarchy of classes of formal languages; more recently, a related view appeared in the framework of recursive function theory in Angluin (1980). In what follows we shall by and large rely on the formulation presented by Wexler and Manzini. In their framework the principle is accompanied by a constellation of auxiliary assumptions, all together belonging to the learning module of the language faculty. A crucial assumption is that the domain-specific learning mechanisms involved are as much a part of the *a priori* baggage of the child as the principles and parameters of Universal Grammar. This modular view of language learning contrasts with views which maintain that no learning theory, not even a domain-specific one, is required to explain the development of parameterized grammars (e.g. see Hyams 1985, 1986).

Linguistically, the subset principle is motivated by Wexler and Manzini's proposal, summarized below, that certain aspects of the binding principles A and B appear to be parameterized in a manner that might create the subset problem. First, consider the contrast shown in these English examples, where the square brackets enclose the governing categories within which the anaphor *himself* must be bound to satisfy principle A (see chapter 2 for the relevant definitions).

(3)a. [John$_i$ criticized himself$_i$]
     [His$_i$ criticism of himself$_i$] was unjustified
     I find [John$_i$ critical of himself$_i$]
  b. *John$_i$ heard [my criticisms of himself$_i$]
     *John$_i$ heard [Mary criticize himself$_i$]
  c. *John$_i$ forced me [PRO to criticize himself$_i$]
  d. *John$_i$ says that [Mary loves himself$_i$]

Whereas only the sentences in (3a) are well formed in English, the counterparts of (3b-d) can also be well formed in some other languages. For example, consider Italian with respect to the reflexive *sè*; the following configurations, the analogues of the illicit English examples in (3b), are grammatical in that language.[4]

(4)a. Alice$_j$ vide [Mario$_i$ guardare sè$_{i/j}$ nello specchio]
     Alice saw Mario look at   Refl in the mirror
  b. Alice$_j$ guardò   [i ritratti di sè$_{i/j}$ di Mario$_i$]
     Alice looked at portraits of Refl of Mario
     'Alice looked at Mario's portraits of Refl'

Contrary to the standard conception of anaphor binding, in (4a) and (4b) the reflexive is bound outside the embedded small clause and the noun phrase, respectively, which should count as governing categories since they contain the anaphor itself, a governor, and a subject. However, if it is assumed that the definition of the governing category for the Italian reflexive *sè* additionally requires the presence of Infl, then the Italian data in (4) can be fully accounted for.

    Likewise, with respect to the Icelandic reflexive *sig* the definition of governing category appears to demand a reference to indicative tense (i.e. the tense of an indicative clause), since this reflexive may also be bound outside infinitival and subjunctive clauses, as shown in (5a) and (5b), respectively.

(5)a. Maria$_j$ skipaði [Haraldi$_i$ að PRO raka sig$_{i/j}$]
     Maria ordered Harald to   shave Refl
  b. Jón$_j$ segir að [Maria$_i$ elski   sig$_{i/j}$]
     Jon says that Maria loves (subjunctive) Refl

    Yet another variant of he definition of governing category is needed to account for the long-distance reflexives found in Japanese, Korean and Chinese, which can be bound even outside an embedded indicative clause, suggesting that only a sentence containing 'root' tense qualifies as their governing category. See the following example with the Japanese reflexive *zibun* (see Cole, Hermon and Sung 1990 for comparable Korean and Chinese examples, but within a different approach to the matter).

(6) John-wa$_j$ [Bill-ga$_i$ zibun-o$_{i/j}$ nikunde iru] to omotte iru
    John   Bill   Refl   hates   that thinks
    'John thinks that Bill hates Refl'

Variation in what is the governing category relative to (a particular lexical item in) a language is also witnessed in relation to pronominals, which, according to binding principle B, must avoid coreference with a c-commanding antecedent within their governing category. So English pronominals tend to be free in much the same governing category in which English anaphors must be bound; on the other hand, Icelandic *hann*, if part of an infinitival clause, may not be bound by an antecedent within the matrix sentence, as illustrated in (7).

(7) *Jón$_i$ skipaði [mér að raka hann$_i$]
    Jon ordered me to shave him

This suggests that the governing category for *hann* requires the presence of tense.

In short, it seems the definition of a governing category has a number of variants, as captured in the following multi-valued parameter, adapted from Wexler and Manzini.[5]

(8) *The Governing Category Parameter*
    γ is a governing category for α iff γ is the minimal category that contains α and a governor for α and
    a. has a subject; or
    b. has an Infl; or
    c. has a Tense; or
    d. has an indicative Tense; or
    e. has a root Tense.

Thus, it would appear that English *himself* (indeed all English anaphors) takes value (a) of the parameter, Italian *sè* value (b), Icelandic *sig* value (d), and Japanese *zibun* value (e). Among pronominals, Italian *lui*, like English pronominals, is said to be associated with value (a), whereas Icelandic *hann* is associated with value (c), and so forth.[6]

The important result from the learnability point of view is that the five values of the parameter (8) generate languages that are contained in each other in a set-theoretical sense. Further, the parameter yields two opposite nesting hierarchies for anaphors and pronominals, quite understandably since the former have to be bound within some designated domain wherein the latter have to avoid being bound.

Let us first consider anaphors. Let L(a), L(b), L(c), L(d), and L(e) be the languages generated under values (a), (b), (c), (d), and (e), respectively, of the parameter. Then L(a) contains all the sentences in which the governing category is characterized by the presence of a subject; so an NP with a subject, an S, or a small clause, all count as governing categories. Given this set of governing categories, it is demonstrable that L(a) is a subset of L(b), since all *sentences* in which an anaphor is bound in one of the governing categories for L(a) will have Infl, and therefore be included in L(b), but L(b) will additionally contain sentences in which an anaphor is bound outside the categories without Infl, namely an NP or a small clause (see examples in 3b and 4). Likewise L(b) is a subset of L(c). All the sentences in L(b) will naturally be a part of L(c), since they will have tense, but L(c) will also have sentences, not included in L(b), in which an anaphor is bound outside a tenseless infinitival clause (cf. 3c). Further, L(c) is included in L(d), as the governing category for the latter should specifically have indicative tense. Although L(a), L(b) and L(c) will be compatible with this specification, they will exclude sentences, perfectly legitimate in L(d), in which an anaphor is bound outside an embedded clause with subjunctive tense. Finally, L(d) is a subset of L(e), which permits long-distance binding even outside an embedded clause with indicative tense. To summarize, L(a) is a subset of L(b), L(b) is a subset of L(c), L(c) is a subset of L(d), and L(d) is a subset of L(e), i.e. $L(a) \subseteq L(b) \subseteq L(c) \subseteq L(d) \subseteq L(e)$.[7]

The logic for pronominals is obviously the opposite of the foregoing. In L(e) pronominals have to be free everywhere. So it will only contain sentences with unbound pronominals, such as (9a) below. As unbound pronominals are not prohibited in any language, L(d) will contain L(e), but will also contain sentences in which pronominals are bound in a root clause, i.e. outside an embedded clause with indicative tense; see (9b). The contrast is illustrated here through English.

(9)a. [John$_i$ says that Pron$_j$ loves Mary$_k$]
   b. John$_i$ says that [Mary loves Pron$_i$]

L(d) is in turn a subset of L(c); because the latter permits not only sentences like (9) with nonbound pronominals in categories with indicative tense, but also those like (10a), in which the pronominal is free in a category with subjunctive tense, but can be bound outside it in the matrix clause. Note that we are continuing to use English for the purpose of illustration, which, on account of restrictions on the use of subjunctive, does not actually contain a sentence like (10a).

(10)a. John$_i$ says that [Mary love (subjunctive) Pron$_i$]
   b. John$_i$ forced me [PRO to criticize Pron$_i$]
   c. John$_i$ heard [my criticisms of Pron$_i$]

Further, L(c) is contained in L(b). All the sentence types illustrated in (9) and (10a) are grammatical in L(b); and so indeed is (10b), in which the pronominal is forced to be free in the embedded clause because it has a (tenseless) Infl, though it can be bound in the tensed matrix sentence. Finally, L(b) is contained in L(a), since L(a) includes sentences like (10c), not included in L(b). In (10c) the pronominal must be free in the bracketed NP, because it possesses a subject, a feature that is criterial for L(a) but not for L(b). Consequently (10c) cannot be permitted in L(b), since the pronominal there is not free in the category possessing an Infl (which is the whole sentence), as required. To sum up, the subset hierarchy for pronominals is: $L(e) \subseteq L(d) \subseteq L(c) \subseteq L(b) \subseteq L(a)$. As is obvious, it is a mirror image of the subset hierarchy for anaphors already described.

If the values of a parameter generate languages that are subsets of one another, then that parameter observes *the subset condition*, formulated as follows in Manzini and Wexler (1987).[8]

(11) *The Subset Condition*
   Given the parameter p with values $p_1, \ldots, p_n$, for every p_i and p_j, $1 \leqslant i,j \leqslant n$, either $L(p_i) \subseteq L(p_j)$ or $L(p_j) \subseteq L(p_i)$.

What this says is that if a parameter p has values p_i and p_j, then either $L(p_i)$ is a subset of $L(p_j)$, or $L(p_j)$ is a subset of $L(p_i)$ (cf. 2a above). Now, given that (11) applies in the case of at least some parameter(s) and that the assumption regarding positive-only evidence holds, it is obvious that an ordering of the values is important to ensure correct fixation of the parameter in one of the possible ways; without such an ordering the danger of the learner being forever trapped in an overgeneral language would be always there. But fortunately the values can be regarded to be naturally ordered by set-theoretical inclusion, assuming that the learner is obliged to explore the values in the ascending order of the subset hierarchy, beginning with the smallest language and moving on to gradually larger languages only when prompted by positive evidence. One can in fact conceptualize markedness in these specific extensional terms, as the following definition shows.

(12) Given the parameter p with values $p_1, \ldots, p_n$, for every p_i and p_j, $1 \leqslant i,j \leqslant n$, p_i is less marked than p_j iff $L(p_i) \subseteq L(p_j)$.

For well-known reasons, this view of markedness necessitates a conservative learning principle, which may be stated as follows.

(13) *The Subset Principle*

Let p be a parameter with values $p_1, \ldots, p_n$, fp a learning function, and D a set of data. Then for every p_i, $1 \leqslant i \leqslant n$, $fp(D) = p_i$ if and only if

a. $D \subseteq L(p_i)$ and
b. for every p_j, $i \leqslant j \leqslant n$, if $D \subseteq L(p_j)$, then $L(p_i) \subseteq L(p_j)$.

The subset principle says that the learning function maps the input data to that value of a parameter which is consistent with the data, and is the least marked, i.e. generates the smallest among the languages compatible with the data. The essence of the principle is a deterministic approach to parameter fixation which works in a strictly monotonic way from the unmarked to the marked choices. More explicitly, assume a parameter p (similar to the governing category parameter) with five values ordered in terms of inclusion. The learning could then proceed as follows. The learner will be presented with data corresponding to one of the languages generated by p. Let the ambient language be $L(p_i)$, the language generated under value p_i of the parameter, for all i ($1 \leqslant i \leqslant 5$). Let D be the data presented to the learner, such that $D \subseteq L(p_i)$. Then either the learner will conjecture $L(p_i)$ in one fell swoop on the basis of D, or he might first guess some less marked language, if one is possible, until at least one positive datum δ appears which is in $L(p_i)$ but not in the wrongly inferred language. That should induce a mind change in the learner, forcing him to move to $L(p_i)$. This means that in principle a small number of less marked intermediary choices may intervene between the initial choice and convergence on the correct value.

Assuming that parameters observing the subset condition do indeed exist, one major implication of the above learning scenario is that, though the learner is operating on a severely prestructured choice space, he is still having to employ an explicit learning procedure, albeit a domain-specific one, which is necessary to ensure learnability. This surely belies the claims (e.g. Hyams 1985, 1986) that linguistic theory is the only acquisition theory we need. Merely being able to understand what is to be learned, i.e. a representational view of the thing to be learned, does by no means always suffice to explain how it is learned.

For the foregoing view of parameter fixation to be formally viable, it is paramount to ensure that the set-theoretical relations in question are indeed well defined. The careful reader will have already noticed some necessary caveats to this effect implicit in the preceding discussion. Firstly, the subset principle and the related assumptions as defined above are meant to apply to each parameter independently of the other parameters of UG. Natural languages may choose the unmarked value of one parameter, but the marked one of another; consequently the subset–superset relations may not hold of whole languages. (Hence the restrictive use of the term 'language' mentioned in note 1.) To illustrate, it would appear that binding theory is further parameterized in relation to the nature of the antecedent by which anaphors must be bound and from which pronominals have to be free. The parameter is named and expressed as follows in Wexler and Manzini (1987).[9]

(14) *The Proper Antecedent Parameter*
    A proper antecedent for α is
    a. a subject β
    b. any element β whatsoever.

It should not be too hard to see that this parameter also observes the subset condition, with $L(a) \subseteq L(b)$. Although English anaphors take the least marked value of the governing category parameter, they are associated with the most marked value of the proper antecedent parameter, as they can be bound by subjects and nonsubjects alike. On the other hand, the Japanese anaphor *zibun* must always be bound by a subject, suggesting that it is associated with the unmarked value (a) of the parameter; however, recall that *zibun* is characterized by the most marked value (e) of the governing category parameter. So, unless the subset relations are computed independently for the two binding parameters, the subset principle and the subset condition would be rendered meaningless. Therefore, the notion of language is idealized to a single parameter to make it possible for a parameter to observe the condition independently of other parameters. In short, the subset principle and the subset condition are not well-defined without the following independence principle, reproduced from Wexler and Manzini (1987).

(15) *The Independence Principle*
    The subset relations between languages generated under different values of a parameter remain constant whatever the values of the other parameters are taken to be.

This formal principle is a special case of the more intuitive concept of parameterization as consisting of a set of essentially independent choices each of which can be made straightaway on the basis of relevant pieces of evidence. The grammar of a particular language results from the interaction of the different choices involved, with individual choices having repercussions throughout the grammar, perhaps giving rise to the appearance of a tightly *pre*structured system of deductively linked parameters. For simplicity, we shall largely focus on the governing category parameter in the rest of the chapter; the reader is referred to Manzini and Wexler (1987) for some discussion of how the two binding parameters defined in (8) and (14) interact.

Just as (15) ensures independence among parameters, (16), taken from Manzini and Wexler (1987), ensures independence among lexical items.[10]

> (16) *Lexical Parameterization Hypothesis*
> The values of a parameter are associated not with particular grammars but with particular lexical items.

This hypothesis introduces lexical conservatism (cf. Baker 1979) in parametric theory, and is needed because it is by no means the case that all lexical items of a similar type in a language are associated with the same value of a parameter. For instance, Icelandic reciprocal *hvor annar*, Italian reciprocal *l'un l'altro*, and Italian reflexive *se stesso* are not correctly accounted for under the values of the governing category parameter associated with the other previously cited anaphors – (d) for *sig* and (b) for *sè* – from these languages. Instead, all of these are characterized by value (a) of the parameter, like the English anaphors. We have already seen that it is also not necessary that the anaphors and pronominals in a language take an identical value of a parameter: so Icelandic *sig* takes value (d), but *hann* takes value (c); likewise although Italian anaphor *sè* is accounted for under value (b) of the governing category parameter, the pronominal *lui* in that language, like English pronominals, is associated with value (a). (This is, of course, not to deny that for some functional or other reasons there may be a tendency among different related lexical items in a language to be parameterized uniformly, as in the case of English.)

4.2 The developmental approach

The formal approach primarily focuses on developing a method of rating parameter values for markedness. However, it does not inevitably follow from that approach that a markedness hierarchy is to be translated into a developmental sequence. In other words, it takes markedness to be a function of an evaluation mechanism determining relative priorities among parametric choices, essentially remaining noncommittal regarding the possibility of the reflection of these choices in real-time acquisition, i.e. in the course of development. Contrarily, the developmental approach considers markedness to be a reflection of the order of emergence. So whatever appears first is *ipso facto* less marked, with the degree of markedness being measured by the incidence of parameter resetting involved. Although the binding phenomena have also been subjected to a developmental mode of analysis in a number of studies (e.g. see Grimshaw and Rosen 1990, Sigurjónsdóttir, Hyams and Chien 1988, and the references cited therein), in the following pages we shall concentrate on Hyams's (1986) study of the null-subject parameter.

4.2.1   Hyams's syntactic analysis

On Hyams's analysis of null subjects Agr (AG in her terminology) is PRO in pro-drop languages; in other words Agr may be optionally specified + PRO in these languages. Agr = PRO licences a *pro* in the subject position, which acquires nominative Case and a θ-role in the manner of a lexical pronoun. In languages like English Agr $\neq$ PRO, whereas in languages of the Italian type, Agr = PRO. Two suppositions are crucial to Hyams's analysis. First, she assumes that Infl, which is the head of S, expands in the following manner.

(17) Infl→(Agr) Aux

Agr is present only in tensed clauses, and is the head of Infl when there is no lexical material in Aux. Aux heads Infl when a modal or an auxiliary appears in it. This alternation of the head of Infl is allowed under the head assignment principles (Hyams 1986: 28). In either case, the head assigns nominative Case to the subject. When Aux is the head it assigns Case by virtue of the feature [+ tense] it contains; otherwise Case is assigned by Agr under feature agreement with the assignee. Agr = PRO forces Infl not to contain any lexical material, since the appearance of any such material would mean government of the Infl node, and thus would be incompatible with the existence of PRO in that position.[11]

Hyams appeals to a slightly modified version of the Avoid Pronoun Principle (Chomsky 1981) in order to explain the lack of lexical expletives in pro-drop languages. On Hyams's view pro-drop languages operate under the Avoid Pronoun Principle, which stipulates that pronouns should be used only when forced for pragmatic reasons, as for contrastive or emphatic effects.

The free inversion of subjects to a postverbal position, according to Hyams (1986), is regulated by an independent parameter (Hyams 1986: 57, n 7, also 157). This parameter, sometimes referred to by her as the Rule-R parameter (comparable to Safir's 1985 free inversion parameter; see chapter 2), is formulated in the manner of Chomsky's (1981) Rule-R analysis. Recall that on this account Rule-R applies either in PF, or optionally both in PF and syntax, with the following grammatical consequences: if Rule-R applies in PF, Agr can govern and assign Case to a subject in the preverbal position only, whereas if it optionally applies in syntax, Agr can govern and assign Case to a postverbal subject as well. In the case of subject inversion, on Hyams's view, the preverbal position is occupied by an empty expletive, namely *ex*, analogous to the lexical pleonastic element that appears in non-pro-drop languages. Note that under this analysis tense remains in Infl and continues to govern *ex* after the application of Rule-R, which affects only Agr; tense is affixed invariably in PF (Hyams 1986: 56, n 5).

4.2.2 Null subjects and linguistic development

Now we turn to the developmental aspect of Hyams's (1986) analysis of the null-subject parameter. Hyams (1986) is an interesting attempt to relate developmental acquisition data to linguistic-theoretic argumentation. On the basis of child language data from English and Italian, Hyams claims that the native child learning English sets the parameter first at the null-subject value, selecting a grammar which is identical to adult Italian and Spanish grammars in this respect, until certain trigger elements in the positive data force him to select the less accessible value associated with English. In other words, Hyams claims that the setting of the null-subject parameter is *obligatorily* noninstantaneous, observing a predetermined ordering of values which must be selected in the prescribed sequence during the course of language development. Primarily motivated by developmental considerations, Hyams's proposal has clear linguistic implications as well. So, Chomsky (1987a) comments that Hyams's proposal constitutes 'an example of a hypothesis about universal grammar deriving from language acquisition studies that might be tested by linguists, rather than the converse, as in the usual practice'.

The fundamental premise in Hyams's approach is that child grammars are structured along the same lines as adult ones, and that they are fully constrained by the principles of UG. They may differ from adult grammars in that the child grammars may take different, perhaps less marked, values of parameters, a possibility that straightforwardly follows from the basic tenets of linguistic theory. But children's competence as it develops from one intermediate grammar to another never strays outside the scope of UG. Reorganization that occurs at each stage strictly observes the permitted parametric variation; in fact each instance of restructuring is an instance of the resetting of a parameter value under the influence of positive data. It is worth emphasizing that Hyams's analysis of pro-drop is susceptible to a 'no-growth' interpretation (see Chomsky 1987a). Hyams herself does not discount a maturational view; she claims that her approach is not incompatible with such a view. For instance, she remarks that child grammars *'though perhaps not fully specified*, will not fall outside the limits imposed by UG' (1986: 5) (emphasis added), and that 'the maturational hypothesis proposed by Borer and Wexler [1987] is not inconsistent with the approach to acquisition adopted in this study' (ibid.: 169). Nevertheless, at least as far as pro-drop is concerned, her view of child grammar is in effect a 'no-growth' one (Chomsky 1987a). It analyses child language as if all the elements it contains are fully realized and identical to adult language, an assumption which among other things entails that the child has a full, but not necessarily correct, knowledge of each component of sentence structure.

Hyams considers the differences between a pro-drop language (Italian) and a non-pro-drop one (English), extrapolates these to child language data from English and Italian, and proposes that early child language (roughly in the age range of 1–3 years) is, in general, a pro-drop language, even if the language being learned is characterized by overt lexical subjects. This is so, she claims, because the pro-drop property is inherently the 'initial' value of the parameter. Thus with respect to this parameter Italian is specified for the initial value, whereas English is not; but in both cases the early grammars are pro-drop. Thus sentences like the ones set out in (18) are ungrammatical in adult English, but according to Hyams they are entirely well-formed in early English, in which Agr = PRO and therefore phonetically null subjects are possible together with overt ones. Pronominal subjects are generally omitted because the child operates with the Avoid Pronoun Principle mentioned earlier.

(18) Shake hands
     See window
     Want more apple

Some other notable characteristics of the child grammar, call it G_1, are: (a) absence of contractible *be* (see (19)), (b) absence of true modals and of their inversion (as in (20), where * is used to indicate non-occurring forms), and (c) lack of lexical expletives; i.e. pleonastic pronouns *it* and *there* (21).

(19) Mommy sleeping
Gia writing
Man making muffins

(20)   I can't wear it *but*
*I can do it
*Can I have it?

(21) Outside cold   ('It's cold outside)
No morning   ('It's not morning')
No more cookies   ('There's no more cookies')

In the early stages modals and auxiliaries in the input data are simply filtered out by the child, since his grammar cannot analyse them. These emerge in child language at approximately the same time as the systematic use of overt pronominal subjects, in step with the resetting of the pro-drop parameter to the non-pro-drop option. Possible exceptions to this are *can't*, *don't*, uncontractible copula, and semi-auxiliaries (*hafta, gonna*). But these are not used productively by the child; their use springs either from misanalysis or from a total lack of analysis (see Hyams 1986 for detail). Take, for instance, *can't* and *don't*; if these were real Infl-based modals, the child would be able to invert them to formulate questions, but this, we know from (20), is not the case. (Note that 'Move Infl' to Comp is blocked unless there is an auxiliary or modal element in Infl.) In respect of the lack of modals early English patterns with Italian, in which modals receive the full range of verbal inflections and are analysable as full verbs. (English modals, contrarily, have a defective morphology.) Recall that in both Italian and early English Agr = PRO, which entails that nothing should appear under Infl, which is headed by Agr in the absence of any lexical content. Moreover, as well as in early English, there is no subject–auxiliary inversion in tensed Italian clauses. Note that this type of inversion is possible in tenseless sentences, but then tenseless sentences do not contain Agr = PRO. Finally Italian, like most pro-drop languages, does not have pleonastic pronouns, a well-attested observation regarding child grammars of English, as the examples in (21) indicate.

Restructuring from G_1 to adult grammar is triggered by certain elements in the input, previously unnoticed and filtered out, which the child begins to perceive and analyse. These trigger elements in particular deserve mention here.

> (22)a. Lexical expletives (i.e. *it* and *there*).
>   b. Infelicitous pronouns (unstressed subject pronouns which are not required by the Avoid Pronoun Principle).
>   c. Modals and *be* in sentence-initial position in yes/no questions.

It is commonly assumed that in the unmarked case pro-drop languages do not have overt pleonastic pronouns (but see chapter 6 for a more complex view). Therefore, when the child begins to discover the identity of these, he or she soon realizes that they would not be possible unless the ambient language was not a pro-drop one. Following a similar logic the use of unstressed subject pronouns not forced by pragmatics will make the child switch to the non-pro-drop option.[12] Finally, sentence-initial modals should help establish that the ambient language contains modals that are generated in Infl, otherwise their movement to the sentence-initial position would not be possible (cf. Guilfoyle 1984). These trigger elements, Hyams proposes, eventually compel the child to a reanalysis of his grammar from $Agr = PRO$ to $Agr \neq PRO$.[13]

Further, Hyams (1986) proposes a general principle which may be invoked to justify why a particular value of a parameter, rather than another, is initial, e.g. why pro-drop, rather than non-pro-drop, is the more accessible option. The criterial factor underlying this principle is the complexity of the grammar attained as a result of a particular setting of a parameter, with a less complex grammar having priority over a more complex one. The principle, called *the isomorphism principle*, is stated in the following manner (Hyams 1986: 162ff).[14]

> (23) *The Isomorphism Principle*
> All else being equal, the least complex grammatical system is the one which allows the greatest degree of isomorphism between the various levels of representation, D-structure, S-structure, PF, and LF.

Assuming, as under the standard analyses, that a pronominal at D-structure is nonlexical, merely being a set of abstract features (person, number, gender, etc.) which become 'visible' at S-structure due to the assignment of Case, it follows that a pro-drop language is more isomorphic than a non-pro-drop one because in it pronominals are (optionally) not lexicalized at S-structure. In a non-pro-drop language, on the contrary, the D-structure and S-structure will necessarily be nonisomorphic due to the obligatory lexicalization of pronominals at the latter.

4.3   Conclusion

The subset principle and the associated assumptions together characterize a very restrictive learning theory for a parameterized language system. It can be taken to be a first approximation of a theory of how parameter fixation could occur, and as such it raises many interesting questions. On the other hand, the developmental approach is proposed to be a theory of how parameter fixation does occur. Conceptually distinct though these are, the approaches under consideration are not mutually exclusive in an absolute sense. Thus, the formal approach exploiting extensive cross-linguistic variation in anaphor and pronominal binding is susceptible of a developmental interpretation; and the null-subject parameter, the historical starting point of the developmental view, is investigated later in the present study from a formal linguistic and learnability viewpoint (see also Saleemi 1988a, 1990, for shorter earlier accounts). However, before proceeding to our own account of the null-subject phenomena we would like to further compare and critically examine the models discussed above; this is exactly what is done in the next chapter.

5 *The scope and limits of the current approaches*

Not surprisingly, several linguistic, learnability-theoretic and acquisitional questions issue from the set-theoretical approach of Wexler and Manzini and from Hyams's developmental approach. Some of these questions are identified, discussed and analysed in the following pages.

5.1 An examination of the formal approach

In some important respects the set-theoretical model of Wexler and Manzini appears to be a step in the right direction. Linguistically, the model has given the idea of a multi-valued parameter a concrete shape. It has also raised interesting questions regarding the way parameters could be related to each other, basically as to how independent the fixing of the one parameter is from that of another. However, one should remember that the set-theoretical approach, as it is presented by these authors, is perhaps more of a *tour de force* than an empirically viable theory; for one thing, it is deterministic in the sense that the environment's role is primarily one-way, i.e. that of providing input, and not backing it up by some form of monitoring of the knowledge acquired in the first instance; moreover, it is far too deterministic to be psychologically convincing and too conservative to be applicable to a wide range of parameters. As a result, it may be necessary to put some empirical flesh on the formal skeleton it furnishes.

By far the most important issues emerging from the set-theoretical approach are the empirical and developmental ones, namely: (i) whether any parameters other than the binding ones, or *even* the binding ones, observe the subset condition, (ii) whether parameters are truly independent of each other, (iii) whether parameters are fixed for individual lexical items or for languages as a whole, and finally (iv) whether linguistic development is influenced and guided by a strictly conservative principle.

76

5.1.1 Syntactic phenomena and the subset condition

We have mentioned before that parameter fixation most probably does not cover all aspects of language learning, learning of lexical items *per se* being a prominent example of nonparametric learning. One can nevertheless presume that parameter fixation does indeed fully determine the properties of a core grammar.[1] Logically the next issue to consider is the extent to which the subset principle explains the full range of cases of parameter setting. Clearly, the principle can be true only insofar as the subset condition turns out to be linguistically justifiable; that is to say, if the values of most parameters, such as they are, yield languages that are nested. However, there is no reason that this should be the case; as noted previously, learning from positive-only evidence is also possible with intersecting and disjoint languages, *regardless* of the order in which the related values are tried. The question to consider, therefore, is to what extent the language-based notion of markedness embodied in the subset condition is viable.

The stronger claim of course would be that all parameters observe the subset condition, and that the subset principle is the only procedure of fixation, with the obvious corollary that if some parameters do not appear to be learnable by this procedure, then perhaps they need to be reformulated or redefined. A weaker hypothesis, on the other hand, would be content with accepting a limited role for the principle, applying it only where it can apply, without much reanalysis or reformulation. The extent to which parameters observe the subset condition is not easy to determine. One problem is that though many parameters have been proposed, those that are generally recognized as such are few and far between. If the notion of parameter is to remain sufficiently constrained, every axis along which languages vary cannot be reduced to a parameter. On the other hand, conservative learning of the sort predicted by the subset principle could also be relevant to several nonparametric types of variation which result in subset relations, and are thus subject to the same type of learnability logic.

Two examples of aspects of grammar apparently compatible with the subset condition are (i) Case adjacency, and (ii) configurationality. Stowell (1981) proposes an adjacency condition on (objective) Case assignment under government, stated in (1), which requires that nothing should intervene between a Case assigner and the Case assignee, say a verb and its complement.

(1) *Case assignment under government*
     In the configuration [α β ...] or [... β α], α Case-marks β, where
  (i) α governs β and
  (ii) α is adjacent to β, and
  (iii) α is [−N].

In the unmarked cases this condition is strictly observed, as in English.
Contrariwise, in some languages certain elements, e.g. an adverbial, are
allowed to disrupt the sequence in some configurations, although it ought
to be kept in mind that the phenomenon is lexically restricted. For
simplicity, we shall assume that Case adjacency follows from a parameter
with two values, one corresponding to strict adjacency and the other to the
lack of it (see Stowell 1981 for a more detailed account). If such a parameter
exists, then it yields two languages one of which is a subset of the other. To
be specific, a non-strict-adjacency language (e.g. French) will be the larger
language, since it will contain sentences not observing adjacency (see the
French example (2a), from Sells 1985) as well as those which do (see the
French example (2b)). On the other hand, a strict-adjacency language like
English will exclude configurations of the type illustrated in (2a).

(2)a. J'aime beaucoup les fleurs
        *I like very much flowers
   b. J'aime les fleurs beaucoup
        I like flowers very much

The following Italian examples, drawn from Stowell (1981), show that
Italian behaves like French with respect to verb–object adjacency.

(3)a. Mario ha letto attentamente un libro
        *Mario has read attentively   a book
   b. Mario legge spesso dei libri
        *Mario reads often books

Likewise, a configurational language (like English) can be considered to
be a subset of a non-configurational language (such as Hindi–Urdu) in the
relevant respect, since the number of word-order permutations allowed in
the latter will increase the number of sentences in it, without excluding
those included in the former. (See Chomsky 1981: 127ff, Hale 1983 on non-
configurationality.)

A more general way to look at the validity of the subset principle is to try
to ascertain its scope by investigating if there is any general linguistic
approach that appears to be conceptually compatible with it. There is
indeed a major strand within linguistic theory, often known as locality
theory (Culicover and Wilkins 1984, Koster 1978; also see note 5 to ch. 2),

which could well be regarded as being the representational counterpart of a conservative procedural approach, such as the set-theoretical learning theory under consideration (Koster 1987: 318ff). The essence of locality theory is that in the unmarked cases linguistic principles are defined over the minimal or local domains, and that in the marked cases the definition of a domain may get extended in various ways, giving rise to parametric variation. So parametric variation could be defined as a specification of different choices of a structural domain over which an otherwise invariant principle applies. The governing category parameter, obviously, is an appropriate example of parametric choice of this kind. For anaphors, the minimal domain, a maximal projection with a subject, is represented by value (a) of the parameter, which gets extended by the successive addition of various opacity factors, namely the presence of Infl, tense, etc., with the most marked value (e) being minimally defined over a root sentence that contains a sentence (i.e. a degree-1 sentence); see (4) where α stands for an anaphor and (a)–(e) depict governing categories corresponding to the values of the parameter.[2] Note that this is only one type of domain extension; see Koster (1987) for an extensive discussion of some other possibilities.

(4)a. $[_{XP} \ldots \text{subject} \ldots \alpha \ldots]$
   b. $[_S \ldots \text{subject} \ldots \text{Infl} \ldots \alpha \ldots]$
   c. $[_S \ldots \text{subject} \ldots \text{Infl} + \text{Tense} \ldots \alpha \ldots]$
   d. $[_S \ldots \text{subject} \ldots \text{Infl} + \text{Indicative Tense} \ldots \alpha \ldots]$
   e. $[_S \ldots \text{subject} \ldots \text{Infl} + \text{Tense} \ldots [_S \ldots \alpha \ldots]]$

However, insofar as locality is a well-defined notion, it is clear that it is not coextensive with the subset condition. For instance, Move-α is a rule whose parameterization would by consensus be taken to rely crucially on some notion of locality, with languages not allowing syntactic movement (e.g. Chinese which according to Huang 1982 lacks Wh-movement in the syntax) representing the local, unmarked option. As the identity of a language with syntactic movement is detectible through observation of relevant positive examples, the notion of locality operative here is compatible with a conservative learning strategy, but one which cannot be described in terms of the subset principle; setting aside echo questions, a language with obligatory syntactic movement in the relevant set of configurations and a language without syntactic movement in the same set of configurations are disjoint. There is a third possibility, exemplified by French (Aoun et al. 1987) in which Wh-movement is *in general optional*. Now this optionality does yield subset relations. How then could one describe the parameterization of Move-α in a fashion consistent across the three possibilities? This will not be possible in extensional terms, since both disjoint and subset languages are yielded. Perhaps the important concept is that of choice, i.e. choice between whether or not movement is allowed, between whether or not movement is optional. The ordering can then be captured in terms of some precise notion of the locality of choice, a notion that will not be a formal notion, but a more linguistic, domain-specific one, which could of course have some formally consistent extensional consequences. (Another alternative view of the ordering of the values of the parameter is outlined in section 7.3.1 below.)

A major problem with the governing category parameter is that the variation it predicts appears to be relatively better motivated for anaphors than for pronominals. Most reflexives, and almost all reciprocals, are associated with the unmarked value (a) of the parameter, as predicted, but pronominals also tend to cluster around the value (a), the most marked for them. In fact, no pronominal associated with the unmarked value (e) is known to exist.[3] Manzini and Wexler (1987) suggest that the anaphors and pronominals in a language are parameterized such that at least one anaphor and one pronominal have complementary or overlapping distribution. This generalization, called *the spanning hypothesis*, explains why pronominals behave the way they do: if pronominals were to take the unmarked value in a language, then the governing categories associated with them could properly include the governing categories related to anaphors, and as a result 'in that language there would be configurations in which it would be impossible to express any binding relations at all' (Manzini and Wexler 1987: 440). According to Manzini and Wexler the spanning hypothesis just 'happens to be true of natural languages as they have actually evolved, but has no psychological necessity, either as part of the theory of learnability or as part of the theory of grammar' (ibid.: 440). This explanation leaves much to be desired. What seems more natural is that the unmarked value for pronominals is the same as that for anaphors, and therefore a view of markedness that does not capture this rather plausible observation is possibly fundamentally misguided. Yet another possibility is that only those pronominals which are bound variables are to be accounted for in binding theory (Montalbetti and Wexler 1985), and that other pronominals are freely indexed at S-structure (Bouchard 1984).

Parameterization of another fundamental aspect of UG, namely the direction of complementation, or for that matter that of θ-role or Case assignment, also yields languages which are disjoint. The null-subject parameter also may not be entirely consistent with the subset condition; see the following chapters for a detailed analysis. We provisionally conclude that subset–superset relations are a superficial reflex of two types of choice mechanisms: (i) those involving optionality (e.g. non-configurationality), and (ii) some of those in which domain extension is implicated (e.g. the governing category parameter). In sum, it appears that the extensional outcome of parameter values is rather varied, ranging over all types of set-theoretical relations.

5.1.2   Independence and lexical parameterization

Independence of parameters from each other and lexical parameterization are two components of the subset approach that together may be seen as a recipe for the fragmentation of linguistic theory. Arguing along these lines, Safir (1987) further points out that the learning model under consideration is so concerned with the avoidance of overgeneralization that it is likely to run into the converse risk of undergeneralization.

It is possible to argue that parameters may in fact be mutually dependent in a systematic fashion. Chomsky, for instance, remarks that due to the 'rich deductive structure' of the theory 'change in a single parameter may have complex effects, with proliferating consequences in various parts of grammar' (1981: 6), and that parameter setting is 'guided perhaps by a structure of preferences and implicational relations among parameters of the core theory' (ibid.: 7). While discussing the subset principle, Chomsky again states that although there may be such general principles that determine how parameters are set, 'There may also be specific principles of markedness relating various parameters, which need not and may not be fully independent' (1986a: 146).

However, as we have mentioned before, independence is not necessarily incompatible with the rich deductive structure of the theory, although it may be advisable to retreat from the notion of independence advocated by Wexler and Manzini, which is probably too strong. Some measure of independence, in a non-subset sense, may indeed be necessary if the idea of parametric choice is to remain theoretically interesting, since too many implicational relations will indubitably destroy the very foundations on which the idea of selective, as opposed to enumerative, learning rests. Although it may be argued that the dependency links among parameters will restrict the class of natural languages in some sense, the significance of such a claim for learnability is far from obvious. Under the theory of principles and parameters the learner is assumed to make individual choices, not to enumerate the whole set of natural language grammars.

Consequently restriction of the class of natural languages is inconsequential so long as the number of choices the learner has to make is not too large. However, it might be that implicational tendencies are not formal constructs of a theory of UG, but may instead be phenomena that are characteristic of particular grammars.

Taken at its face value, the lexical parameterization hypothesis might be an optimal solution to the learnability of anaphors and pronominals, but it is not clear that it will generalize to other aspects of language in any consistent or otherwise significant way. Take the head-direction parameter. It does not seem reasonable to maintain that the fixation of the head-direction parameter takes place on an item-by-item basis; the undergeneralization problem Safir (1987) is worried about is just round the corner! A speculative solution is that parameter fixation is lexical in relation to closed-class functional items, but language-wide otherwise. So, one would like to assume that the head-direction parameter operates on categories of X-bar syntax, rather than on individual lexical items. On the other hand, the closed-class lexical items (e.g. anaphors and pronominals), being small in number, may well be parameterized individually.

5.1.3   Is acquisition conservative?

Throughout this chapter we have in general ignored the implications of the subset approach for natural child language acquisition data (see Wexler and Manzini 1987 for some discussion specifically relevant to binding principles). It would be appropriate to mention that in principle evidence from child language data may provide empirical counterevidence to the approach if it turns out that children do often overgeneralize before successfully retreating to smaller languages. Pinker (1986) claims that whereas in a number of cases overgeneralization does not occur, in others it is well attested in acquisition data, leading to the paradoxical conclusion that children are both conservative and nonconservative at the same time. Some pertinent examples (adapted from Pinker 1986, where the relevant original sources are cited), not necessarily relatable to any corresponding parameters, are given below.

> (5)I *Conservative*
> (a) It is known that children do not make too many word-order errors. Children learning fixed word-order languages never go through a stage where their language has a free constituent order. However, the converse appears to be true.

(b) Children learning English do not invert main verbs in questions. Moreover, they do not invert auxiliaries or semi-auxiliaries which are typically not inverted in adult language.

(c) In child language the canonical sequence of auxiliaries is preserved, and they are never wrongly inflected.

II *Nonconservative*

(a) At early stages children typically underdistinguish between various morphological distinctions, e.g. those between genders. So children may use the same inflection for both the genders. (See Hyams, to appear, for a parametric view of the acquisition of inflection.)

(b) Children often overgeneralize the productive rules of verb sub-categorization, e.g. dativization, passivization, the causative formation, denominalization, etc.

(c) Failure to invert subject and auxiliary in English Wh-questions, and the incorrect inversion of these elements for the quasi-Wh word *how come*, are not uncommon.

In view of such apparently contradictory evidence, it is possible that acquisitional tendencies by themselves can have no decisive role in establishing whether children are truly conservative learners.

5.2   A critical look at the developmental approach

Hyams (1986) makes two explicit claims which are essential to the main thrust of her approach. First, Hyams's bold hypothesis is that linguistic theory (as manifested in the principles-and-parameters approach) is the only language learning theory that is needed; viewed from this perspective, the learning simply consists of a search for the correct parameter values from among the possible ones. Second, Hyams presents an even stronger hypothesis, that linguistic theory is also a theory of language development, so that the values of a parameter must be chosen one after another in a prescribed order, all but the last one of which can be abandoned in the course of acquisition. Not unexpectedly, as demonstrated in the following pages, the resulting model of language acquisition can hardly stand up to theoretical scrutiny, much less explain a wider range of developmental evidence (the interested reader is referred to Radford 1990 for a parallel critique).

5.2.1   Theoretical problems

One major potential flaw in Hyams's analysis of pro-drop, at least intuitively speaking, is that it regards that value as developmentally prior which intuitively appears to be less restrictive. A pro-drop language admits of optionality of lexical subjects; therefore presumably it is less restrictive than the case where lexical subjects are obligatory. This has led many researchers to claim that a non-pro-drop language is a subset of a pro-drop one in the relevant respect (e.g. Berwick 1985). Hyams's isomorphism principle is meant to provide an alternative notion of restrictiveness, but it does not do justice to the problem in hand, largely because the D-structure and S-structure in a pro-drop language cannot be consistently isomorphic, but are so only in an optional sense. This surely diminishes the relevance of the principle to the pro-drop parameter.

Furthermore, there is a good deal of inconsistency between certain assumptions required under Hyams's approach and her avowed aims. For instance, although she is careful not to declare that the initial setting is the unmarked value (1986: 156ff), it is difficult to understand the distinction if the initial value is defined as the one 'given by UG in advance of experience with a particular language' (1986: 8), a definition that comes very close to being a possible definition of an unmarked value. One assumes that Hyams's intention is to keep apart markedness and developmental precedence, but that is not of a piece with her general approach, which seems to be based on the assumption that developmental grammars 'can provide empirical support for particular principles of UG' (1986: 2). Some of Hyams's syntactic assumptions lead her into theoretical difficulties not dissimilar to the one just outlined. Thus, Guilfoyle (1984) points out that the head-assignment principle violates X-bar theory, in that it allows the head of Infl to oscillate between Agr and lexical modals, between nominal and verbal character. As a rule the nature of a projection is uniquely determined by its head, which may not be variable, otherwise projections cannot be considered to be systematic hierarchical expansions of specific zero-level categories. Even more important in the present context are the consequences of this syntactic problem for acquisition: as Hyams acknowledges, the unique relationship between a head and its projections is possibly an important factor whereby 'the child may deduce hierarchical structure from a surface string' (1986: 28); consequently, positing a category without a unique head is not advisable from an acquisitional viewpoint either. In any case, whether or not theoretical and developmental phenomena actually coincide, Hyams's approach represents but one way of relating developmental grammars to linguistic theory. That alternative developmental accounts of the null-subject parameter are possible is demonstrated in the following section.

5.2.2 Maturational alternatives

A developmental view of parameter setting, of which Hyams (1986) is historically the most influential example, is not compulsory; it probably is not correct either. For the purpose of her analysis of pro-drop, Hyams (1986) essentially considers the child's linguistic competence to be complete in relation to adult competence, not appreciably differently from the continuity hypothesis (Pinker 1984). Further, she takes it for granted that only one of the variant values is operative within the child's competence at any given stage of development. Alternative conceptions of the process are possible if the presence of subjectless sentences in child language is variously accounted for either (a) in terms of performance factors (Bloom 1990), or (b) if one appeals to learning factors, arguing for example, as does one major strand in the work of Valian (1989, 1990), that both the values of the parameter are available to the child from the outset, and that it takes some time and effort on his or her part to sort out the evidence and to select the correct one, or (c) if, due to linguistic factors, the child's competence is regarded as being immature, causing frequent omission of different elements, such as subjects (Guilfoyle 1984, Lebeaux 1987, Radford 1988a, 1990; see also Borer and Wexler 1988). For familiar reasons, below we shall set aside (a) and (b), and largely concentrate on the linguistic factors, and show how maturational alternatives alone render Hyams's view untenable.

Insofar as the child learner does move from one parametric choice to another in the course of acquisition, it should in principle be possible, though by no means necessary, to relate parametric theory to developmental facts in a systematic way. However, it is far too obvious that child language differs from adult language in more than just the particular parameter values selected; in several nontrivial respects child language appears to lack elements which are an essential feature of adult competence. To elaborate, recall that under Hyams's analysis a developmental grammar G_{s-n} is distinct from an adult grammar G_s (= steady-state grammar) if the two grammars differ with respect to the values they take of a given parameter p. However, there is another possible way in which the two grammars could differ. Suppose that the difference can be traced to the absence of a certain category in G_{s-n}; in other words, G_{s-n} is not just different but incomplete (see chapter 3 for a discussion of so-called 'growth' theories of language acquisition). Also suppose that the absent category is vital to the setting of parameter p, such that without it the question of the parametric choice is totally irrelevant. Under such circumstances, it would be perfectly legitimate to describe G_{s-n} as a grammar that has no value for p, rather than as one having a value of p different from that underlying G_s. On such a non-parametric view of syntactic development, parameter setting would not necessarily be expected to proceed in developmental stages corresponding to different values of p. Instead, it would in fact be possible for the learner to speedily converge on the correct value at some appropriate point in development, without first having to embrace a provisional value. If such a view is plausible, then the set of ordered choices associated with a parameter should not be regarded as a developmental scenario, but merely as an evaluation metric employed by the learner to fix a value, a process that may or may not have any discernible developmental consequences.[4]

One nonparametric alternative to Hyams's account is presented in Guilfoyle (1984), who asserts that although the child grammar of English is indeed characterized by frequent absence of overt pronominal subjects, the pro-drop parameter *per se* is not relevant to this developmental phenomenon. The reason why the child resorts to the use of null subjects, Guilfoyle maintains, is that his or her grammar is not specified for tense; hence the absence of tense endings and modals in child language. (Notice that Hyams's account does not explain that, roughly at the stage when children produce sentences without overt subjects, inflections for tense are also systematically absent.) Since tense assigns nominative Case to the subject, the subject in child grammar is Caseless, and therefore it cannot be realized in a nominative position. Guilfoyle further proposes, following Gruber (1967), that when lexical subjects are used they appear in a topic position. Thus the early grammar of English differs from adult grammar not with respect to a parameter value, but in virtue of the absence of a grammatical feature, i.e. tense, and the resultant inability of Infl to Case-mark the subject. This assumption, Guilfoyle says, is supported by evidence from Italian child language data as well, because even in early Italian the inflectional endings on verbs do not reflect tense, but are merely a realization of Agr features, with the productive use of past tense inflection emerging much later (around the age of 3 years). Reasoning along similar lines, Lebeaux (1987) suggests that in child language Infl is not generated in its canonical position, but is adjoined to the verb, and is thus not able to assign Case to the subject, with the result that lexical subjects may or may not appear.

Radford's (1988a, 1990) extensive proposal, in part related to the possibility of null subjects in early child language, is in much the same vein.

Based on a naturalistic study of a number of monolingual children acquiring English as their first language, it claims that the grammar of two-year-olds is projected entirely from lexical-thematic categories (i.e. A, N, V, P), and does not contain functional categories such as D(eterminer), I(nfl) and C(omp), which, it is posited, emerge only at the later stages of acquisition. As the nature of subjects in early child language is primarily related to the I system, we shall not have anything to say about the question of the lack of C or D systems. As far as the I system is concerned, in Radford's view there is overwhelming developmental evidence supporting the hypothesis that it is nonexistent in early child grammars, and that, like the small clauses in adult language, children's clauses are projections of lexical categories only, having the following structure.

   (6) $[_{XP}$ (NP) XP]   (where X = N, A, V, P)

The assumption that early English has lexically headed rather than I-headed clauses can account not only for the presence of null subjects but also a whole array of other empirical facts. Radford states that in his child language data characteristics like the ones listed in (7) are attested consistently.

   (7)a. Use of independent nonfinite sentences.
      b. Absence of infinitive Infl *to*.
      c. Lack of inverted auxiliaries.
      d. Possible lack of VP, the complement of Infl, in independent sentences.
      e. Absence of tense.
      f. Lack of systematic agreement.
      g. Absence of nominative Case (and indeed of Case in general).
      h. Free omission of subjects.

Predictably, Radford maintains that (7h), which is of primary interest here, stems from the absence of Infl, a fact all other properties (7a–g) patently point towards. (As in Hyams 1986, the early modals, e.g. *can't*, *don't*, are considered to be unproductive and therefore not an indication of the existence of Infl.) In particular, an obvious consequence of the lack of Infl is that nominative Case cannot be assigned. Recall that, although subjects are licensed by the Extended Projection Principle, it is nominative Case that makes subjects visible at PF, that is, forces the presence of *lexical* subjects at that level. Radford presents evidence to the effect that nominative subjects are not available in children's grammar, which often allows *objective* subjects (see the examples below, showing a lack of nominative/objective contrast).

(8) Me got bean.
    Him asleep.
    Her gone school.

It is, in fact, maintained that children's grammar is in general Caseless, with the result that the principles of Case theory, such as the Case Filter, are not operative in it. The absence of Case in children's grammar should mean that *pro* can occur freely in their speech,[5] which, according to Radford, is indeed the case; thus, *pro* objects are as common as *pro* subjects.[6] Platzack (1990) presents evidence from early Swedish corroborating the foregoing proposal about early English.

So, if it is not at all unreasonable to consider the possibility that child language at early stages simply mimics pro-drop because of the absence of certain enabling features and categories, then we can maintain Hyams's (1986) observation that early child grammar may systematically lack overt subjects, without accepting her explanation of the phenomenon – that child language differs from adult language precisely as one natural language differs typologically from another.[7]

5.3   Discussion

The subset approach ensures learnability from positive-only evidence. In fact, as Berwick (1985) points out, it also obviates the need for invoking indirect negative evidence where the latter does appear to be relevant. However, overall it appears that the approach is far too strong to be universally viable. It is more likely that the learning and linguistic principles underlying the language faculty operate and interact in terms of relations which are not purely formal.

In conclusion, it seems clear that there are many parameters whose values, given the way these are standardly formulated, do not conform to the subset condition. Whether these can be reanalysed to do so is, of course, a moot question, which needs to be resolved. As a step in that direction, in the chapters to follow we undertake a detailed review and reanalysis of the null-subject parameter and of its implications for acquisition.

Hyams's (1986) work has contributed many insights to the study of acquisition and learnability. However, we suspect that her analysis of pro-drop in child language is on the wrong track. A major flaw in her approach is that no compelling reason is given why one value of the null-subject parameter, rather than the other, should be the one that the child initially adopts. For that matter, she does not convincingly justify in the first instance why parameter setting should be compulsorily noninstantaneous (cf. Cinque 1989), a hypothesis that is probably as unreasonable as the instantaneity assumption of Chomsky (1965) translated into developmental terms. Recall that in the previous chapter we assumed that, given a learnability-theoretic ordering of its values, a parameter can be provisionally fixed at a value which is less marked than the target value, but that this does not have to be necessarily the case. In other words, we are suggesting that a parameter value may be developmentally prior only if it is more accessible than the target value in terms of a well-defined learnability metric. Does Hyams's account fit this condition?

The answer is no. There is no learnability logic underpinning Hyams's (1986) developmental conclusions. Given Hyams's linguistic analysis, the pro-drop parameter generates languages which partially intersect, as a pro-drop language would contain sentences with null subjects, not contained in a non-pro-drop one, and the latter would contain sentences with overt pleonastic subjects, in general excluded from languages of the former type. So her formulation of the parameter, as she notes herself, does not create a learnability problem; the pro-drop setting has no logical priority over the non-pro-drop one, since either setting may be determined by positive evidence regardless of which choice is considered to be initial, or unmarked.[8] In sum, Hyams does not offer much in the way of a learnability explanation as to why her claim about the priority of the pro-drop option should be considered correct. In chapter 7 we argue that the null-subject parameter, as formulated in chapter 6, does create a learnability problem, and that the unmarked end of the learnability metric is the non-pro-drop one, rather than the pro-drop one.

It is possible to argue that the learnability arguments we have presented above can be overruled on empirical grounds. That is, it might be that Hyams's view just happens to be empirically correct, for which there is as yet no real explanation. However, plausible maturational alternatives, such as the ones offered by Guilfoyle (1984) and Radford (1988a, 1990), considerably weaken the motivation behind Hyams's (1986) analysis. Thus, it is not the case that Hyams's explanation of the relevant facts of acquisition is the only one available; most probably it is not even the best one among the possible alternatives.

6 *The distribution and variety of null subjects*

In this chapter the licensing and parametric mechanisms underlying the null-subject parameter are reanalysed, in large measure relying on data previously reported in some of the vast literature on the topic (see Jaeggli and Safir 1989b for a state-of-the-art survey and references). The resulting formulation of the parameter is considered from a learnability point of view in the following chapter. Various approaches to the licensing and identification (i.e. interpretation) of null subjects are critically reviewed, leading up to a different view of the licensing and the parametric variation. The key feature of our account of the licensing is that null subjects are held to primarily follow from the optionality of the assignment of Case by Infl (cf. Bouchard 1984, Rizzi 1986a, Safir 1984, 1985). Moreover, following Rizzi (1986a) and Jaeggli and Safir (1989a), we consider the identification of the referential content and features of null subjects to be formally separate from their licensing. Consequently, in much of this chapter we concentrate on the licensing, assuming that an appropriate identification mechanism (see Jaeggli and Safir 1989a for a review) would be available once the licensing convention is in place.

Further, under our analysis the parameterization is considered to be characterized by greater diversity. As pointed out in the previous chapter, the parameter in question has been cited as evidence both for and against the subset principle. To recapitulate, it has been claimed that, in the relevant respect, a language generated by the pro-drop option includes a language generated by the non-pro-drop option (e.g. see remarks in Berwick 1985: 291–3). Conversely, it has been argued that the two types of languages partially intersect, since a pro-drop language does not have sentences with overt expletive (or pleonastic) subjects, whereas a non-pro-drop one does not contain sentences with null subjects (Hyams 1986). However, in this chapter it is demonstrated that neither of the two claims appears to be valid, as the binary-valued formulation of the parameter underlying them may not be descriptively adequate; subsequently, an alternative multi-valued formulation is tentatively proposed.

A crucial prerequisite to what follows is the view that, although only two types of subjects (referential and expletive) are traditionally acknowledged, in fact three types of subjects are found in natural languages. The three types are distinguished from each other by their respective referential and thematic properties. Thus, in addition to the fully referential subject with an R-index, we further identify two nonreferential (i.e. pleonastic) types, namely nonarguments and quasi-arguments. This distinction, due to Chomsky (1981), may be described as follows. A nonargument is an expletive subject which is obligatorily construed with a postverbal NP or CP, e.g. see *there* in the existential construction (1a) and *it* in the extraposition structure (1b).

(1)a. [There] is [a man] at the door
   b. [It] is clear [that Mary is very clever]

A quasi-argument is the expletive subject of atmospheric–temporal predicates. A weather predicate, illustrated in (2a), typifies atmospheric predicates; (2b) represents an example of a temporal predicate.

(2)a. It is raining
   b. It is rather late

Quasi-arguments, not nonarguments, can stand on their own; as mentioned previously, these latter always need to be backed up by a postverbal NP or CP. Moreover, nonarguments always occur in clauses whose verbs do not assign an external θ-role, whereas the predicates of quasi-arguments tend to assign a minimal 'atmospheric–temporal' θ-role to their subjects.[1] The typology of subjects suggested in this paragraph is summarized below.[2]

(3)	R-index	θ-role
a. Referential argument	+	+
b. Quasi-argument	−	+
c. Nonargument	−	−

(3a) and (3b) together are sometimes referred to as argumental or thematic subjects, and (3b) and (3c) as nonreferential subjects. Needless to remark, all of these, when appearing as lexical NPs, must be Case-marked, as required by the Case Filter or the Visibility Condition; a lexical nonargument may thus be regarded as merely a spell-out of nominative Case.

6.1   The function of rich inflection

It has been frequently argued that the presence of rich verbal inflection is the major factor determining the availability of *pro* subjects. That some correlation between the two properties does exist is supported by evidence from various 'mixed' null-subject languages, e.g. Pashto (reported in Huang 1984), Hebrew (Borer 1984), the Bani Hassan dialect of Arabic (Kenstowicz 1989), West Flemish (Bennis and Haegeman 1984), and Irish (McCloskey 1986, McCloskey and Hale 1984),[3] not to mention the familiar cases of full-fledged null-subject languages such as Italian and Spanish. To give an example, Huang (1984) reports that Pashto, a split-ergative language, has a rich agreement system, but one which is manifested differently in present and past tense constructions. In the sentences characterized by the present tense, the verb agrees invariably with the subject. In the case of past tense configurations, however, subject–verb agreement is possible only with intransitive verbs; with transitive verbs the agreement is between the verb and the object. The interesting fact, for the present purposes, is that in Pashto both null subjects and objects can appear, but just in case the null element agrees with the verb.

On the face of it the condition of dependence between a rich enough inflection and subject pro-drop appears to be quite strong, though it is by no means uniform in terms of the detail and range of its application. However, the study of a wider range of languages reveals that this condition is more or less irrelevant to several cases. For instance, French has a rich person–number agreement system, but it is a non-pro-drop language. Mainland Scandinavian languages, e.g. Swedish, do not allow null subjects, the putative reason being the lack of marking of person and number in them; this is contrasted with Insular Scandinavian languages (namely, Icelandic and Faroese), which possess an articulate agreement system, and which are therefore pro-drop, but the problem is that only pleonastic subjects can be omitted in them (see Platzack 1987). German, another richly inflected language, allows pro-drop in an even more limited sense than Icelandic and Faroese, in that only nonarguments are allowed to be null (Safir 1984, 1985). (See section 6.3.3 for relevant examples.)

Various explanations for such limited availability of null subjects have been offered. Safir (1984, 1985) maintains, somewhat counterintuitively, that underlyingly German is a null-subject language in the same sense as Italian, but one in which null thematic subjects are not admitted on account of the absence of a 'major clitic paradigm' in the language, which would ensure proper identification of null subjects; on this view quasi-arguments are considered to be thematic, hence their inability to remain null. Similarly, Jaeggli and Safir (1989a) attribute the lack of thematic pro-drop in some V/2 languages (e.g. German, Icelandic, etc.) to the failure of identification of null subjects in them. These languages are characterized by an obligatory verb-fronting rule, called *Verb Second* or *V/2*, that moves the finite verb from within VP to the second position in all declarative root clauses (some examples appear below in section 6.3.3). The crucial assumption underlying Jaeggli and Safir's (1989a) proposal is that in V/2 languages the tense and Agr components of Infl are distributed in two different nodes – namely Comp and Infl respectively – rather than one, as is usually believed. On their view Agr can identify a null subject only if it is contained in a Case-assigning category, and Infl does not qualify as such a category in the absence of tense; as a result the identification of thematic null subjects by Agr is blocked in the languages under consideration. However, since pleonastics are inherently devoid of any thematic content, they do not require to be identified, and may therefore be omitted.

Although the foregoing proposal seems to be plausible, it is not without problems. The hypothesis that some property of V/2 languages is responsible for the restriction of pro-drop to nonthematic subjects does not correctly explain the difference among languages in the availability of null quasi-arguments and null nonarguments. Icelandic and Faroese, like other Scandinavian languages, also exhibit some variation of the V/2 effect, and therefore should pattern with German in respect of the possibility of null subjects. However, as already noted, they allow both quasi-arguments and nonarguments to drop, in contrast with German in which only nonarguments can remain null. Thus, it would appear that any attempt to explain limited pro-drop, as in German and Icelandic, on the grounds of inaccessibility of Agr is likely to be riddled with inconsistencies.

In view of such evidence it might appear that rich inflection is a necessary, but not a sufficient, condition for pro-drop (Jaeggli and Safir 1989a, Lasnik 1990). However, in some languages inflection does not appear even to be a necessary condition. It is known that languages such as Chinese, Japanese and Korean allow null subjects unproblematically, although they do not possess any system of agreement at all. In fact in these languages empty pronominals are freely possible in the object position as well (see Hasegawa 1985 on Japanese, and Huang 1984, 1987, 1989, and Xu 1986, on Chinese). Evidently, languages like Chinese cannot have identification by means of coindexation with a rich Agr. Presumably, in Chinese the identification may involve pragmatic processes, and is dependent on two different nonlocal mechanisms. For obviative null (variable) subjects it has been proposed that they are coindexed with a discourse-bound null operator in a pre-S position, and for null subjects coreferential with a c-commanding NP in a higher clause, it is maintained that the higher NP serves as the antecedent, perhaps through the mediation of the local empty Agr node (Huang 1984, 1989, Jaeggli and Safir 1989a). In essence, a similar account is available for Japanese (Hasegawa 1985).

6.2   The separation of licensing and identification

One conclusion that can be drawn from the foregoing discussion is that pro-drop and rich inflection are formally separate, which is the view explicitly adopted in Rizzi (1986a) and Jaeggli and Safir (1989a) (also see Jaeggli and Hyams 1988, Shlonsky 1990). Rizzi (1986a) argues that licensing and recovery of content are characteristically independent processes in the theory of grammar. Thus, PRO is licensed by the Projection Principle (or by the Generalized Empty Category Principle; Chomsky 1981), but it acquires its content by means of control mechanisms. Likewise, NP-trace and Wh-trace are sanctioned by the ECP (by lexical government, to be precise), whereas it is through the formation respectively of A-chains and A'-chains that their referential content is fixed. Analogously, it follows that the licensing of null subjects is independent of the various mechanisms whereby their ϕ-features are identified; null subjects appear to be licensed by a Case-governing head, as will be discussed in the following pages.[4] In general, licensing is predominantly syntactic and is exercised through a government-type relation. On the other hand, the recovery of content usually takes place on the LF side, by means of a binding-type relation. In a similar vein, Aoun et al. (1987) argue that the ECP, viewed as a disjunctive condition consisting of a lexical government component and a coindexing component, is a spurious generalization, redundantly combining two distinct types of locality requirement; one structural and operative at PF, the other indexical and applicable at LF. Let us illustrate the separation of licensing and identification of null subjects more concretely by outlining and analysing the two accounts mentioned above, i.e. the ones proposed by Rizzi (1986a) and Jaeggli and Safir (1989a).

6.2.1   Case-government as the licensing factor

Rizzi (1986a) suggests the following general licensing schema for pro-drop that is intended to account for the occurrence of null objects as well as null subjects.[5]

(4) *The licensing schema*
   pro is Case-marked by X_y°.

Here X represents a designated Case-marking head of type y that can license a null argument, and y may range over one or more members of the class of licensing heads, i.e. Infl in the case of null subjects, and V and P in the case of null objects. Languages differ in respect of what can count as a licensing head. Under Rizzi's (1986a) analysis identification is conceived of as a nonstandard type of binding, termed head binding, consisting of binding from the licensing head. Head binding, comparable to other binding-type relations, e.g. control and the formation of A- and A'-chains, is distinct from the licensing of a null category, and is embodied in the following convention.

(5) *The identification convention*
   Let X be the licensing head of an occurrence of *pro*: then *pro* has the grammatical specification of the features on X coindexed with it.

In the case of Infl-licensed *pro* in Italian, (5) coindexes the agreement specification on Infl with the null subject, in accord with the usual assumptions regarding strong construal with a rich Agr.

Some Italian data involving clausal verb complementation is crucial to Rizzi's account (see the examples in (6)–(8), and (19)). In Italian the feature specification is in general sufficiently rich. As a result the tensed complements of most verbs allow null subjects freely, whether referential (6a), quasi-argument (6b), or nonargument (6c); this is so because both person and number specifications are morphologically marked in the contexts under consideration.

(6)a. Ritengo [che *pro* sia simpatico]
   'I believe that (he) is nice'
   b. Ritengo [che *pro* sia troppo tardi per S]
   'I believe that (it) is too late for S'
   c. Ritengo [che *pro* sia probabile che S]
   'I believe that (it) is likely that S'

Not so in the case of some marked infinitival constructions in which the auxiliary moves to Comp and assigns nominative Case to the subject position. Here referential *pro* is not possible because the person specification is lacking.

(7)a. *Ritengo [essere *pro* simpatico]
    'I believe to be (he) nice'
  b. Ritengo [essere *pro* troppo tardi per S]
    'I believe to be (it) too late for S'
  c. Ritengo [essere *pro* probabile che S]
    'I believe to be (it) likely that S'

Finally, in complement small clauses the range of null subjects is even further reduced due to the lack of any feature specification. Consequently, all null subjects other than the nonargument *pro* are excluded.

(8)a. *Ritengo [*pro* simpatico]
    'I believe (him) nice'
  b. *Ritengo [*pro* troppo tardi per S]
    'I believe (it) too late for S'
  c. Ritengo [*pro* probabile che S]
    'I believe (it) likely that S'

So the logic appears to be that, although *pro* is formally licensed in all the above contexts, its actual appearance is dependent on an appropriate identification requirement. Thus, referential pro-drop requires stronger agreement in the form of person–number markings, whereas nonreferential pro-drop either requires weaker agreement in the form of number specification (for quasi-arguments), or no agreement whatsoever (for nonarguments). So, a consequence of this type of approach is that one can continue to regard the null-subject parameter as a minimal binary difference, and totally shift to the identification or recovery component the burden of explanation of the vexing diversity of the null-subject phenomena, a move that we consider to be undesirable for a number of reasons.

It is obvious that an assumption of the separation of licensing and recovery is not entirely unproblematic in the presence of conflicting evidence indicating either a strong relationship between pro-drop and a rich Agr, as in the case of Italian, Spanish, etc., or none at all, as the languages which do not have an Agr component, e.g. Chinese and Japanese, illustrate. It is likely, though, that this relationship is specific to *particular* languages, or perhaps that it is determined by a separate parameter (Huang 1984, Jaeggli and Safir 1989a, Rizzi 1986a). So Huang (1984, 1989) suggests that in some languages (Pashto, Italian, etc.) the two properties are grammatically interdependent, whereas in others (e.g. Chinese) the process of recovery is pragmatic (cf. Jaeggli and Safir 1989a). Rizzi (1986a) speculates that identification *via* agreement with Infl is

parameterized, so that different languages adopt different options, sometimes fully, sometimes partly, and sometimes not at all. If operative in a
given language, the recovery mechanism overrides the consequences of the
null-subject parameter whenever the retrieval of certain designated
feature(s) of the empty subject from overt affixation on Infl is not possible.
On this view the realization of pro-drop, though not its causation, is
directly dependent upon the extent to which pronominal features are
recoverable from the overtly realized context.

6.2.2   The morphological uniformity hypothesis

Jaeggli and Safir propose a novel, though 'somewhat programmatic'
(1989a: 2), account of null subjects. Their analysis depends crucially on the
following definition of morphological uniformity.

> (9) *Morphological uniformity*
> An inflectional paradigm P in a language L is morphologically uniform iff
> P has either only underived inflectional forms or only derived inflectional
> forms.

Notice that 'inflectional forms' is a blanket term here; it refers to inflection
for tense, mood, aspect, person–number agreement, etc. It is the uniformity
of affixation, not its nature, that is under consideration. The null-subject
parameter, according to these authors, is as expressed in (10).

> (10) *The null-subject parameter*
> Null subjects are permitted in all and only languages with morphologi-
> cally uniform inflectional paradigms.

Compare the following paradigms from English (11a), French (11b),
Spanish (11c), Japanese (11d), and Chinese (11e), taken from Jaeggli and
Hyams (1988) and Jaeggli and Safir (1989a).

(11)a.	to talk	infinitive	
	talk	present 1sg, 2sg, 1pl, 2pl, 3pl	
	talk-s	present 3sg	
b.	parl-e	infinitive ('to talk')	
	parl	present 1sg, 2sg, 3sg, 3pl	
	parl-õ	present 1pl	
	parl-e	present 2pl	
c.	habl-o	'I speak'	1sg
	habl-as	'you (sg) speak'	2sg
	habl-a	'he/she speaks'	3sg
	habl-amos	'we speak'	1pl
	habl-áis	'you (pl) speak'	2pl
	habl-an	'they speak'	3pl

d. yom-ru   'read-present'
   yom-ta   'read-past'
   yom-anai   'read-neg'
   yom-eba   'read-conditional'
   yom-oo   'let's read'
   yom-itai   'want to read'
   yom-are   'was read'
   yom-ase   'make read'
e. xihuan   'like'

First consider English and French, both non-null-subject languages. The English paradigm is neither rich in terms of person–number distinctions nor uniform. French, though richly inflected, has non-uniform morphological paradigms; for example, the present tense form is underived. Now consider Spanish, a null-subject language; Spanish is both richly and uniformly inflected. Finally, the Japanese paradigm is uniform, but lacks number–person markings; yet Japanese is a null-subject language. Chinese, another null-subject language, is like Japanese in being without number–person inflections; but unlike Japanese Chinese has no inflections whatsoever for tense, mood, etc. Nevertheless, according to (9) Spanish, Japanese, and Chinese are all languages which have uniform paradigms.

As we are aware, a major assumption of Jaeggli and Safir's analysis is that identification and licensing are separate mechanisms, and that a rich Agr is involved in the former, but not in the latter. Under Jaeggli and Safir's account, however, the licensing is determined by the uniformity of inflectional paradigms in a language. If a language either contains inflectional paradigms that uniformly consist of derived verb forms, i.e. forms distinct from stems, or has no derived forms at all, then that language is predicted to be a null-subject language: Italian and Japanese fall into the former subcategory, and Chinese into the latter. On the other hand, if a language contains mixed paradigms, including both derived and underived (nondistinct from stem) forms, then it will not allow null subjects: both French and English fit this category.

The question immediately arises as to why languages like German, which do have uniform morphological paradigms, do not allow the full range of null subjects. As previously discussed, Jaeggli and Safir believe that in German (and indeed in all languages showing V/2 effects) the pro-drop is prohibited due to the failure of identification of the grammatical features of the subject. We have already mentioned that the idea is difficult to make precise, particularly with respect to the two types of pleonastics.

Further, Jaeggli and Safir propose a licensing condition that is merely based on a correlation; they have nothing to say as to why morphological uniformity should be related to the possibility of a null subject. The only reason why inflections can be relevant to pro-drop is if they serve to further distinguish tense/mood inflections for person and number; but then we simply have to return to the idea that identification *is* licensing. In any case, the condition of morphological uniformity appears to be a gross generalization. As Jaeggli and Safir acknowledge, the Mainland Scandinavian languages are morphologically uniform, but they do not allow any null subjects. It remains to be seen to what extent the notion of morphological uniformity is a useful construct.

6.3 Case and visibility

What is then responsible for the licensing of *pro* in the subject position? Building on the insights gained from Bouchard (1984), Hornstein and Lightfoot (1987), some of the papers in Jaeggli and Safir (1989b), and Rizzi (1986a), we intend to argue that the possibility of a *pro* subject in finite clauses is related to the Case and visibility requirements, which also underlie the distribution of PRO, a type of null category found alike in pro-drop and non-pro-drop languages in the subject position of nonfinite clauses.

6.3.1 PRO and *pro*

Chomsky writes that 'control structures are essentially the same whatever the value of the pro-drop parameter' (1981: 326). Thus, as the following examples taken from Jaeggli and Safir (1989a) indicate, Spanish and English contrast with respect to the possibility of null subjects in tensed clauses (12a), but not with respect to null subjects in control structures (12b).

(12)a. (Él) siempre habla de   sí mismo
        *(he) always talks about himself
    b.   Juan intentó [PRO hablar de   sí mismo]
         John tried   [PRO to talk about himself]

As is evident from these examples, in both languages a PRO subject appears in infinitival clauses, which, like subjects in general, is required by the Extended Projection Principle (Chomsky 1982), or by the rule of predicate-linking (Rothstein 1983), but only in Spanish-type languages is a *pro* subject optionally allowed in tensed clauses.

Let us first try to ascertain what determines the distribution of PRO. Recall that usually the distribution of PRO is considered to follow from binding theory, in particular from the PRO theorem (see chapter 2). To recapitulate, under binding theory it is assumed that PRO is a pronominal anaphor. Since as a pronominal anaphor it would be subject to the contradictory requirements of both principles A and B, and hence could not be both bound and free within a governing category, it follows that PRO can appear only in an ungoverned position, namely as the subject of infinitival and gerundive clauses. So Chomsky (1981; also see 1982: 104–5, n 40, 1986a: 117) and Lasnik and Uriagereka (1988: 48ff) maintain that fundamentally lack of government determines the occurrence of PRO. However, our contention is that the nonavailability of Case in the subject position of nonfinite clauses, rather than the PRO theorem, is primarily responsible for the occurrence of PRO (cf. Borer 1989, Bouchard 1984, Hornstein and Lightfoot 1987, Huang 1989, Manzini 1983).[6] This obviously entails that lack of government is not responsible for the phenomenon, as is generally believed; note that Hornstein and Lightfoot (1987), Borer (1989), and Huang (1989) all argue that PRO may be governed; in fact, Borer (1989) and Huang (1989) go so far as to claim that the two empty categories *pro*/PRO are in essence indistinguishable and should therefore be collapsed into a single entity. Now, insofar as Case assignment occurs under government, government must undoubtedly be involved in the process. As it happens, the configurations of government and Case are identical in most cases, and therefore the mechanism crucially involved in a phenomenon is not easy to distinguish. As an attempt to conclusively settle this issue falls out of the scope of the present discussion, we shall confine our discussion to only those configurations that are relevant to the task in hand, and shall in general continue to assume that PRO is licensed as a result of lack of Case, or of Case-government (Aoun 1985). In the following pages some evidence (mainly from English) is provided in support of this assumption, as its implications for the licensing of *pro* subjects are significant.

In infinitival structures Infl is nearly universally incapable of assigning Case to the subject, since it is usually devoid of Agr (a known exception is some Portuguese structures; see Raposo 1987), and always devoid of tense. Regarding the mechanism of Case assignment, we are assuming, following Koopman (1984), that nominative Case is assigned by a verbal Infl, i.e. by an Infl that contains a verb which has moved into it to acquire tense and/or agreement features. Koopman (1984) reasons, contrary to the usual assumptions (e.g. Chomsky 1981), that neither tense nor Agr is directly involved in the assignment of nominative Case. Instead, the presence of either of the two, or both, elements in Infl forces the verb to raise into Infl (cf. Chomsky 1989, Pollock 1989), which can then assign Case to the subject position. As all lexical NPs are required to have Case (by the Case Filter or by the Visibility Condition), the result is that a lexical subject cannot appear in the subject position of infinitival clauses, unless it is Case-marked from a pre-S position. Thus, in English nonfinite constructions (e.g. the embedded clauses in 13a, 15a) a PRO *can* be replaced by a lexical subject if the subject position of the infinitival complement is governed and Case-marked, either by a prepositional complementizer (as in (13b), (15b)) or by the matrix verb (e.g. see (14c)).

(13)a. [PRO$_{arb}$ to read] would be nice
   b. For [him to read] would be nice
   c. *[Him to read] would be nice
(14)a. *I believe [PRO to be unpredictable]
   b. *I believe for [Harry to be unpredictable]
   c. I believe [Harry to be unpredictable]
(15)a. I must arrange [PRO to go to New York]
   b. I must arrange for [Mary to go to New York]
   c. *I must arrange [Mary to go to New York]

Evidently, (13c) is ill-formed due to the absence of any Case-assigner. Furthermore, (14a) is ungrammatical because verbs like *believe* render the subject position of the infinitival complement transparent for government, hence for Case assignment – unlike *arrange*-type verbs which do not (see (15a)) – and (14b) is illicit on account of the fact that *believe*-type verbs do not allow a prepositional Case-assigner to intervene, again in contrast with *arrange*-type verbs which do (see (15b)), but which cannot themselves (exceptionally) Case-mark a subject in the constructions in question, as the ungrammaticality of (15c) instantiates. A similar alternation of PRO with a lexical NP is manifested in the case of certain gerundive subjects optionally marked with nominative Case in some exceptional manner:

(16)a. PRO having arrived late, Mary started work immediately
   b. John being absent, Mary decided to take over

Further, if lexical pleonastics are a mere spell-out of Case, as it is plausible to assume, then they should not be able to appear in the Caseless position under consideration (17a), unless they are 'externally' Case-marked (17b), nor should a PRO be able to replace them, as indeed appears to be the case (17c).

(17)a. *[It to rain now] would be nice
    b.   For [it to rain now] would be nice
    c. *For [PRO$_{arb}$ to rain now] would be nice

The argument is extendable to genitive Case assignment. Either a Case-marked lexical NP appears in a position where genitive Case may be (optionally) assigned (18a), or a PRO will occupy the same position (18b).

(18)a. I like [John's/his singing]
    b.   I like [PRO singing]

As English is a non-pro-drop language, it only affords a two-way comparison between PRO and lexical subjects. Now let us put the pattern of occurrence of these two in the context of a pro-drop language, e.g. Italian, in which *pro* subjects are also possible. Consider these examples (drawn from Rizzi 1986a) of Italian infinitival structures of the type which begin with the complementizer *di*.

(19)a.   Ritengo [di PRO essere simpatico]
         'I believe to be nice = I believe that I am nice'
    b. *Ritengo [di *pro* essere simpatico]
         'I believe (him) to be nice'
    c. *Ritengo [di *pro* essere troppo tardi per S]
         'I believe (it) to be too late for S'
    d. *Ritengo [di *pro* essere probabile che S]
         'I believe (it) to be likely that S'

Our approach correctly predicts that, due to the lack of Case, only a controlled PRO can appear in the subject position in these examples. Note that *pro* is not possible in this context; it seems it can appear only in contexts where Case *is* available. Comparably, in the Italian infinitival constructions in which the auxiliary element in Comp assigns nominative Case to the subject, no referential null pronominals are possible, as shown above in (7); however, since Case is assigned PRO is also excluded. For obvious reasons, the option to have a null subject in the corresponding tensed clauses is freely available, as already illustrated in (6).

6.3.2   Optionality of Case

In general, it is an established fact that *pro* can occur only in those contexts in which overt Case-marked NPs can appear. Thus, Rizzi (1986a) asserts that *pro* can only be licensed by a Case-assigning head, which is Infl in the case of a subject *pro*. We can draw many different conclusions on the basis of this generalization. To begin with, we can hypothesize that *pro* is Case-marked just like lexical NPs (e.g. Chomsky 1982: 86, Hyams 1986: 32–3). Alternatively, it can be stipulated that in null-subject constructions nominative Case is absorbed by Infl (Rizzi 1986a), or that it is simply not phonetically realized (Safir 1985). None of these assumptions is straightforwardly consistent with the view that Case requires a nonvariable NP to be phonetically realized at PF (Bouchard 1984, Fabb 1984). A further possibility is to maintain that, although Case can be assigned in the positions where *pro* occurs, in fact for some reason it may be blocked. Compatible with the hypothesis that NPs are lexicalized at PF only if they have Case, and that escaping Case entails an empty category at PF, such a view may regard pro-drop as involving optional blocking of Case in finite clauses, with the licensing condition for the null-subject parameter stated as follows.

(20) *Licensing Condition*
The assignment of Case by Infl may be optionally blocked.

It would then appear that there is a crucial parallel between nonfinite constructions in general and finite constructions with null subjects, in that in both cases the possibility of null subjects follows from Case theory; both the null categories in question, i.e. PRO and *pro*, are made possible on account of lack of Case at S-structure; hence the fact that they are not visible at PF and are not lexicalized. The difference is that in tensed clauses this possibility follows from the nonassignment, rather than complete absence, of Case. Indeed lack of Case appears to be responsible for the occurrence of yet another type of empty category, namely NP-trace. The object position of passive and raising verbs is known to be Caseless; in both cases the D-structure objects have to move between D-structure and S-structure to the higher subject position where they can be Case-marked. Strictly speaking, the trace so created is not a null category, because it appears in a chain that is visible at S-structure by virtue of containing a Case-marked position. In short, it seems plausible that, with the well-known exception of Wh-traces, empty categories are by and large created by the nonavailability of Case.

Keeping the foregoing discussion in view, (20) would appear to be a valid formulation. However, apparently, it is problematic in one important respect; it violates the Visibility Condition, in that it blocks the assignment of Case on the LF side as well as on the PF side. It is generally assumed that Case is instrumental in ensuring visibility at both PF and LF: just as arguments cannot have a phonetic matrix without Case at PF, they cannot be assigned θ-roles at LF, and thus may not be interpreted, unless they are

Case-marked. Recall that by the Visibility Condition θ-role assignment at LF can occur only if an argument is Case-marked (Aoun 1985, Chomsky 1981, 1986a). So, if a *pro* reached LF without Case, it would not be visible for θ-role assignment at that level. Indeed this logic is applicable to PRO as well, which is usually thematic but is always without Case, and is known to constitute an embarrassing exception to the Visibility Condition. We suggest a solution to the problem which is in line with the visibility requirements at both PF and LF.

Adopting the framework developed in Hornstein and Lightfoot (1987), we propose the following twofold definition of the Visibility Condition; (21a) is concerned with visibility in PF, and is simply a restatement of the Case Filter, and the disjunctive statement of visibility in LF, i.e. (21b), is adapted from the work already cited (see Hornstein and Lightfoot 1987: 46, 49, etc.).

> (21) *Visibility Condition*
>   a. To be visible in PF, an NP must be Case-marked.
>   b. To be visible in LF, an NP must either be Case-marked, or appear in an obligatory position.

Thus, a position that is obligatorily projected, such as the subject position of a clause, does not have to be Case-marked; this would render any empty category in this position (*pro*/PRO), with or without Case (according to Hornstein and Lightfoot 1987 PRO need not be governed, but it may not be Case-marked), visible in LF, whereas an NP in an optional position, patently, cannot make an appearance in LF without Case. In the presence of this revised view of LF visibility, it should be obvious, the Licensing Condition in (20) no longer violates the visibility requirements, and can therefore be taken to be tenable.[7]

To sum up, we hypothesize that null subjects are formally made possible by the optionality of Case. This Licensing Condition, together with identification through some (perhaps language-particular) means, determines whether a language will allow null subjects.

6.3.3   Parametric variation

Much like the traditional approaches, the Licensing Condition (20) differentiates null-subject languages from non-null-subject ones on a binary basis. It is notable that a multi-valued parameter, such as the one proposed by Wexler and Manzini, makes it possible to directly capture a wider range of variation. On the other hand, a binary formulation that is intended to account for the same range of variation must somehow explain away part of the attested diversity. However, an interesting view, which is the one prevalent at present (e.g. Rizzi 1986a), is that perhaps all parameters are intrinsically binary-valued, and when some of them do appear to have multiple values, the causes lie in the interaction of parameters within a particular language. Though seemingly attractive for various reasons, this viewpoint, we suspect, is not necessarily preferable to, or even clearly distinguishable from, admitting multi-valued parameters in the theory.

Theory-internally, such a view implies that parameters can massively nullify each other's triggering conditions, with one parameter almost undoing the effect of another one, a supposition that is likely to run up against considerable descriptive and learnability problems. Many of the former have already been touched upon, while as far as learnability considerations are concerned, this kind of approach would be tantamount to a conspiracy for the suppression of relevant evidence, which conceivably might slow down the process whereby the language learner is supposed to pick the correct value of the parameter. This underscores the point that the major motivation behind a parameterized theory of grammar is to guarantee learnability, a key assumption being that the parameterization consists of discrete, independent choices. The theory, though, does not rule out the possibility that parameters interact, or that the degree of mutual *functional* or *interactive* compatibility (in some sense that can be made precise) between different parameters may be rather strong; hence the tendency in null-subject languages with a rich Agr to depend on identification through overtly realized ϕ-features. Further, a many-valued analysis should be of greater advantage in determining learnability if the corresponding binary analysis requires the postulation of many additional grammatical mechanisms in the system, the exact consequences of which may appear to necessitate some intricate deductive reasoning on the part of the learner. So after all the availability of fewer choices might not be such a great advantage from a learning point of view.

Considering (20) to be essentially correct, we shall now explore the possibility of revising the null-subject parameter to encompass more than two types of languages. Is the null-subject phenomenon diverse enough to warrant an expanded typological analysis? The following crosslinguistic data suggest that such an analysis is quite plausible.

First consider these German examples.

(22)a. *(Es) troff
     it   dripped (Safir 1984)

b. Heute regnet *(es)
    today rains   it
    'it's raining today' (Travis 1984)
c. Heute sind (*es) zwei Kinder gekommen
    today are   two children come
    'today there came two children' (Travis 1984)

Unlike Italian and Spanish, in German pro-drop is available only in a very reduced range of contexts. Referential pro-drop is not allowed at all (22a). A nonargument subject, *ceteris paribus*, is obligatorily omitted in many constructions (22c), but a quasi-argument subject must always be retained (22b). In other words, in German argumental subjects must never be omitted (Safir 1984, 1985, Travis 1984). (At this point we do not comment on the apparently obligatory nature of the omission of the nonargument, an issue that will be taken up in due course.)

The German facts, as implied above, are not quite as simple, and therefore deserve some comment. Specifically, it is not the case that lexical nonarguments can be freely dispensed with. Consider the following examples.

(23)a. *(Es) wurde ein   Mann getötet
        there was   a-Nom man   killed
    b. *(Es) scheint, daß er kommt
        it   seems   that he comes (Safir 1984)

In neither of these examples is the expletive subject *es* allowed to drop, presumably on account of the V/2 constraint. Let us analyse (23a) and (25a–b) as (24), adopting the framework proposed in Chomsky (1986b), while essentially following the view incorporated in Travis (1984).

(24)

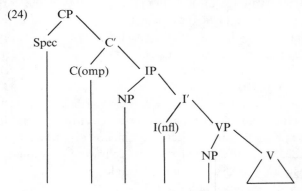

(23)a.   es wurde$_j$ ein Mann getötet e$_j$
(25)a. Gestern wurde$_j$ (*es)   ein Mann getötet e$_j$
    b.   daß (*es)   ein Mann getötet wurde

In these examples *es* appears in the position of the specifier of IP, and in subject-initial sentences the second position for the finite verb is Infl. The finite verb lands in Comp only if an element other than the subject (a temporal adverb in the case of 25a; also cf. 23b) moves to the first position in the sentence, which is Spec (of CP). Returning to the question of when expletives in German must not be dropped, we assume that in German subject-initial sentences the subject must appear in order to fulfil the V/2 constraint, which according to Travis (1984) follows from a parameter whereby the lexically filled Comp in German is a proper governor. When there is a complementizer in Comp, it properly governs its complement IP. Further, it also governs the head of IP, namely Infl, under the stipulation that if an element properly governs a maximal projection it also properly governs its head (see Chomsky 1986b). In subject-initial root clauses the finite verb has to move to Infl since, in the absence of a complementizer in Comp, this empty position must be filled to satisfy the ECP. Likewise, in non-subject-initial sentences such as (25a) the preposing of an element to the Spec of CP triggers V-movement into the ungoverned Comp position. On the other hand, in embedded clauses the finite verb need not move to Infl, which is properly governed, and can therefore remain empty, again in keeping with the ECP. Thus, the parameter in question accounts for the V/2 effect, the well-known fact about German in which the location of the finite verb alternates between the D-structure sentence-final position in embedded clauses and the second position in main clauses.

Consequently, one can predict that in German nonarguments can be omitted as long as they are not required by an independent parameter governing V/2 effects; according to Safir, 'for some speakers this prediction is roughly borne out' (1984: 216). However, one should note that some further restrictions, of a relatively less systematic nature, appear to exist that counteract the possibility of a null subject in certain cases; see Safir (1984, 1985) and Travis (1984).

To return to the variation in the range of pro-drop, according to Travis (1984) Yiddish represents yet another type, as these examples indicate.

(26)a. Haynt hot　 *(es)　alts　　gegesn
　　　 today has　　 it　　all　　eaten
　　　 'it has eaten everything else today?'
　　b. Haynt geyt (*es) a regn
　　　 today goes　　　rain
　　　 'it's raining today' (Travis 1984)

As in German, referential pronouns are never dropped in Yiddish (26a).
But no nonreferential pronouns, including quasi-arguments (26b), can
appear overtly. With respect to nonreferential drop, Malagasy (Travis
1984) and Insular Scandinavian languages, namely, Icelandic and Faroese,
pattern with Yiddish (Platzack 1987); see these Icelandic examples.[8]

(27)a. Rigndi (*það) í gær?
       rained it in yesterday
       'did it rain yesterday?'
   b. í dag hafa (*það) komið margir málvísindamenn hingað
      today have there come many linguists   here
      'today there have arrived many linguists' (Platzack 1987)

Finally, as is well known, Italian permits referential pro-drop as well as
nonreferential pro-drop, as demonstrated below (also see the above
examples in (6)).

(28)a. (Io) vado   al cinema
       (I) go   to the movies
       'I go to the movies'
   b. Sembra che Gianni sia molto infelice oggi
      seems that John is very unhappy today
      'it seems that John is very unhappy today'
   c. Piove molto durante il   mese di febbraio
      rains a lot during the month of February
      'it rains a lot during the month of February' (Hyams 1986)

In this respect Spanish, Portuguese, and many other null-subject languages
resemble Italian. Clearly, a revision of the traditional binary view of pro-
drop is in order. Rizzi (1986a) speculates that the (partial) typology of the
world's languages with respect to Infl-licensed *pro* is as follows, with
languages lacking Agr possibly representing an additional type.

(29)a. no occurrence of *pro* (English)
   b. *pro* = nonargument (German)
   c. *pro* = nonargument and quasi argument (Yiddish)
   d. *pro* = nonargument, quasi-argument, and referential argument (Italian)

However, as noted above, Rizzi (1986a) adheres to a binary-valued
formulation of the parameter, suggesting that the reduced range of pro-
drop in some essentially pro-drop languages may be a result of the
language-particular interaction of the null-subject parameter with an
independent parameter that regulates the recovery of pronominal features
in a piecemeal fashion, as described earlier.

We suggest that a more effective way to characterize the null-subject phenomenon, in part following the typological variation noted by Rizzi (1986a; also see Travis 1984), is to posit a wider range of parameterization. Therefore, under our analysis the null-subject parameter is reformulated as a multi-valued parameter, which may now be restated as follows, combining the effects of (20) and (21) with the consequences of the linguistic variation exemplified in the preceding pages.

(30) *The null-subject parameter*
    Σ may optionally remain invisible in PF, where Σ represents a class of subjects containing:
    (a) θ; or
    (b) nonarguments; or
    (c) nonreferential arguments; or
    (d) any arguments whatsoever.

English, French, and Swedish are associated with value (a) of the parameter, allowing no null subjects. On the other hand, German takes value (b), that permits only nonarguments to be omitted, requiring all argumental subjects to be lexically expressed. Yiddish, Malagasy, Icelandic and Faroese take value (c), that allows the omission of quasi-arguments as well as nonarguments, i.e. all nonreferential subjects. Finally, languages like Italian and Spanish (and probably also those like Chinese and Japanese) are associated with value (d), under which any subject, referential or nonreferential, may remain null.[9]

Whereas Rizzi's (1986a) proposal does not have much to say regarding languages without Agr, Jaeggli and Safir's (1989a) account is in theory coextensive with our account in terms of empirical coverage. Both attempt at accounting for the distribution of null subjects in languages lacking an Agr component as well as in languages containing this component. Also, as has been pointed out, they agree on the separation of identification from licensing. Clearly though, they differ with respect to the analysis of languages which are pro-drop only in a partial sense; the present account explains the existence of these languages by spacing out the parametric variation, whereas Jaeggli and Safir attempt to account for such cases in terms of the failure of identification. The major difference, of course, is that in the present analysis pro-drop is attributed to the optionality of syntactic Case, in contrast with Jaeggli and Safir who consider morphological uniformity to be the basic licensing condition. Although it is not our intention here to defend our analysis at length, we would like to point out that, theoretically, the evidence weighs in favour of the present view of licensing in at least one major respect: the causal link between Case and PF visibility is well motivated, naturally extending to the distribution of PRO.

The null-subject parameter as stated in (30) gives rise to two problems, a descriptive problem and a learnability problem, to the former of which we first turn. Is the null-subject parameter (30) descriptively adequate? It is apparent that if the typology of languages outlined under (29) is indeed accountable for in terms of parametric variation, then (30) has an edge over other formulations of the parameter, which cannot directly explain cases represented by German and Yiddish. There is an apparent problem, though. (30) predicts that pleonastic pro-drop will be optional, just like referential pro-drop.[10] However, whereas referential pro-drop is in general optional, nonreferential pro-drop seems to be mandatory in most pro-drop languages, with a few (possibly marked) exceptions, e.g. Irish (Travis 1984: 231ff), Welsh, and substandard Hebrew (Borer 1984: 216).[11] Practically, then, the pro-drop option with respect to pleonastics might be no more than a Hobson's choice. But there appears to be a simple solution to the problem.

In the spirit of Chomsky's (1981) Avoid Pronoun Principle, the absence of lexical pleonastics in many pro-drop languages can be ultimately attributed to their pragmatic infelicity. Travis remarks: 'Unlike referential pro-drop, pleonastic pro-drop appears to be obligatory ... I assume that in both cases, pro-drop is optional. Referential pronouns may be used for emphasis. Since this is senseless in the case of pleonastics, they will never appear' (1984: 229) (cf. Hyams 1986). Even syntactically, if the pro-drop property indeed springs from the optionality of Case at S-structure, then the avoidance of pleonastic elements is understandable as they will tend not to appear in syntax merely as a spell-out of Case, possibly as a reflex of their elimination in LF, as Chomsky (1986a) suggests; note that under Chomsky's (1986a) analysis an expletive is replaced in LF, *via* an application of Move α, by the postverbal referential complement to which it is linked. In sum, it can be assumed that since pleonastic subjects are nonreferential, they would be superfluous, and thus might not, or might have ceased to, exist in a null-subject language. What we are suggesting is that there could be more or less fortuitous gaps in languages (though perhaps not in their grammars) that might (at least in part) be ascribable to the lack of semantic and pragmatic usefulness.

We can thus indirectly account for the lack of expletive subjects in most pro-drop languages, and one could still claim (30), pragmatically qualified, to be formally correct. In any event, this maximally general statement of the parameter may be required for languages in which nonreferential pro-drop is in fact optional in many configurations, obviating the need to explain away such cases by labelling them as highly marked; see these examples from Welsh, Irish, Faroese, and Urdu.

(31) *Welsh* (Awbery 1976)
  a. Mae hi'n hwyr
    is it   late
    'it is late'
  b. Mae'n hwyr
    is   late

(32) *Irish* (Travis 1984)
  Bhí (sé) crcidte ariamh againn go dtiocfadh   an slanuitheoir ar ais
  was it believed ever   at-us Comp come(Condit) the Saviour   back
  'we had always believed that the Saviour would come again'

(33) *Faroese* (Platzack 1987)
  a. Heani   var (tað) ikke langt til garðarnar
    from-there was there short way to the-farms
    'from there it was a short way to the farmsteads'
  b. Nú er (tað) heilt   víst at   John hevur sligið Mariu
    now is it   obvious   that   John has   beaten Mary
    'it is obvious now that John has beaten Mary'
  c. í dag eru (tað) komnir fleiri málvísindamen higar
    today has there come   many linguists   here
    'today there have arrived many linguists'

(34) *Urdu*
  a. (yi) maaloom hotaa hai ki   voh jaa chuka hai
    it   seem   Asp is that he go Asp   is
    'it seems that he has gone'
  b. (yi) vaazeh hai ki   us ne jhoot bolaa   thaa
    it obvious is that he Erg lie   spoken was
    'it is obvious that he had lied'

Nevertheless, due to the irregular distribution of pleonastics in languages, the shortfall in the data available to the learner leaves us with a learnability problem, particularly in the total absence of any kind of negative evidence, as is explained in the following chapter.

7 *Augmented parameter fixation:* pro *subjects and learnability*

The null-subject parameter, as formulated in the last chapter, defines four types of languages, i.e.: (a) those totally without null subjects, (b) those in which nonarguments alone are allowed to be null, (c) those permitting all pleonastic subjects (nonarguments or quasi-arguments) to remain phonetically empty, and (d) those in which all manner of subjects may be null, with the optionally null pleonastics often displaying the tendency not to be overtly realized. As a result, the parameter raises the interesting question of the relationship between parameters and the languages they generate, and of the resulting implications for learnability, with renewed force. It affords an example of the intricate connection between parameter values and the corresponding languages, in particular of a mismatch between the two, perhaps suggesting that parameters do not, strictly speaking, generate languages, but only fix the maximal bounds within which languages can be realized. This possibility is analogous to the familiar case of potential and actual forms, of structures that are predicted to be well formed by a grammar but that do not exist (cf. Pinker 1989: 98ff). This gives rise to some inconsistency between the training instances available to the learner and the relevant generalization in the grammar. The parameter in question illustrates that this state of affairs is possible in a parametric theory as well, resulting in a comparable learnability paradox that we are going to consider in this chapter. As the data the child will get may not exactly be the data he will expect under the parameter, the problem to resolve is how the child infers the presence of gaps in the ambient language in the absence of any negative information. In more general terms, the question is how the learner deals with *partial* generalizations in the target grammar.

7.1   Identification of the parameter values

In answer to the above paradox, we shall suggest that at least the following two modes of identification of the properties of an ambient language are involved in the process of acquisition.

(1)a. Positive identification
  b. Exact identification

As will be demonstrated in the following pages with reference to the null-subject parameter, (1a) is a selective mechanism; it is designed to yield the knowledge of the correct value of the parameter, and is sufficient when the maximum grammar-evidence correspondence is obtained. On the other hand, (1b), an observational strategy, may be required if the input language, though essentially reflecting the underlying grammar, yet fails in certain (limited) instances to obey it. (Note that our use of the term 'exact identification' is different from Osherson et al.'s 1984, 1986a, and therefore is not to be confused with the latter.) The process of the setting of parameter values, so coupled with some observational learning, is what we term *augmented parameter fixation*.

7.1.1 Positive identification

It is plainly obvious that in principle the four values of the null-subject parameter (stated as (30) in the previous chapter) should generate languages which form a subset hierarchy, as each value potentially increases the set of well-formed structures allowed by the parameter. That is, if lexical pleonastics were in general optional, then the situation obtained would be compatible with the monotonic model of parameter fixation proposed by Wexler and Manzini, indicating that the parameter could be straightforwardly fixed on the basis of positive-only evidence. This indeed might be more or less correct in relation to those languages in which the pro-drop of pleonastics is optional to some degree; there will be no learnability problem insofar as overt pleonastics exist. However, due to the nonappearance of overt pleonastics in many null-subject languages, we cannot be sure that each of these languages will actually fall into a subset hierarchy in respect of the parameter. Under such circumstances the subset principle cannot be regarded as an effective learning procedure. This points to the possibility of a projection problem, relevant only to those languages that contain gaps resulting from the nonexistence of overt pleonastics. The best way to spell out this problem explicitly is to assume the 'worst case', that is, the situation in which overt pleonastics are absent from all types of null-subject languages. In such a state of maximal deviation from the parameter, the set-theoretical relations between the languages will be as follows.

Let L(a) be the language related to value (a) of the parameter; likewise

L(b), L(c), and L(d). Then it is obvious that L(a) and L(b) will partially intersect, as L(a) contains sentences with overt nonarguments, which L(b) will not have, and L(b) contains sentences with null nonarguments that are excluded by L(a). Next consider L(c). L(c) has sentences with null quasi-arguments, not included in L(b), whereas L(b) has sentences with overt quasi-arguments that will not be contained in L(c). Therefore L(b) and L(c) will also intersect. Now consider L(d). L(d) will be coextensive with L(c) with respect to the nonpresence of nonreferential subjects, but it additionally admits referential null subjects. Consequently, L(c) ⊆ L(d). In short, the set-theoretical profile of languages that will emerge is rather mixed, incorporating *both* subset and intersecting relations, not strictly in keeping with what the subset principle and the related assumptions predict.

Given the way the values of the parameter reflect a gradual decrease in restrictiveness, and the fact that the relations among languages may involve at the least one subset–superset relation (i.e. that between L(c) and L(d)), it is obvious that the order in which the values are supposed to be inspected by the learner remains an important consideration. A total absence of any subset–superset relations would have made the question of order irrelevant, as criterial evidence distinguishing all of the four values from each other could have been available no matter in which particular order the values were considered. The question then is how to impose an ordering on the set of values associated with the parameter. Note that it is still possible to consider that the values of the parameter are ordered in terms of markedness just as dictated by a subset hierarchy, as in theory the parameter is compatible with the subset condition. However, that may not be desirable, since it has been shown that although the languages associated with different values of the parameter can fall into a subset hierarchy, they do not do so in relation to a significant number of cases. Alternatively, one can define the inclusion relations among values, rather than extensionally (i.e. among languages generated by these values), a possibility that follows naturally from the internal structure of the parameter. The markedness hierarchy and the learning procedure can accordingly be redefined.

Recall that the set of null subject types under the four values progressively enlarges from value (a) to value (d): the set of null subjects under value (a) of the parameter is ∅; the set of possible null subjects under value (b) consists of nonarguments only; the set of possible null subjects under value (c) has as its members quasi-arguments as well as nonarguments; and the set of possible null subjects under value (d) contains nonarguments, quasi-arguments, and referential arguments. In other words, in this specific sense value (d) includes value (c), value (c) includes value (b), and value (b) includes value (a). The following condition is proposed to determine markedness among parameter values that are so related.

> (2) *Markedness condition.* Given a parameter p with values $p_1, \ldots, p_n$, for every p_i and p_j, $1 \leqslant i, j \leqslant n$,
> a. p_j includes p_i iff the set of categories to which p_i applies is a subset of the set of categories to which p_j applies; and
> b. p_i is less marked than p_j if p_j includes p_i in the sense of (a).

The intuitive idea behind (2) is that markedness is a function of certain internal properties of language, rather than of the external properties of particular grammars (cf. Chomsky's 1986a distinction between E-language and I-language). The chief criterion for markedness, accordingly, is subset relations among sets of categories affected by the values, rather than among the sets of strings they generate. Although in certain respects (2) and Wexler and Manzini's subset condition are practically equivalent, (2) differs from the subset condition and the related subset principle in one important respect: since it is not conceived of in terms of languages, psychologically it could be more plausible. Wexler and Manzini's learning module appears to presuppose quite complex computational abilities on the part of the learner, who may have to compute different subset hierarchies for different lexical items of the same type, and who must further establish distinct hierarchies for pronominals and anaphors (see Safir 1987 for some discussion of this issue). Whether or not the child is endowed with such abilities is of course a moot point, but it seems to us that a learning module that depends rather heavily on language-related definitions cannot be considered realistic so long as an alternative more reliant on the nature of grammars involved is available.

Much as we may desire it, we do not expect (2) to be the only criterion for determining markedness. There may be other notions of markedness which, though different from (2), are essentially compatible with it to the extent that they are firmly grounded in grammatical constructs. Later in this chapter we shall see that (2) can be shown to be relevant to the binding parameters of Wexler and Manzini as well.

Given that (2) applies at least in the case of some parameters, the learning can be easily taken care of by a rather general procedure, defined in (3), that takes (2) as one of the metrics of markedness, and correspondingly inspects the parameter values in the ascending order of markedness. This learning procedure will not, at least in the cases when (2) or a similar condition applies, need to observe extensively the languages associated with these values.

> (3) *Learning procedure.* Given a parameter p with values $p_1, \ldots, p_n$, let $L(p_i)$ be the language generated under value p_i of the parameter p, let f_P be the learning function for p, and let D be a set of data. Then for every p_i, $1 \leqslant i \leqslant n$, $f_P(D) = p_i$ iff
> a. $D \subseteq L(p_i)$, and
> b. p_i is the least marked value which is consistent with D.

(3) formalizes the learning procedure, which says that the learning function f_P maps the set of data D onto a value p_i of parameter p if and only if D is a subset of $L(p_i)$, the language generated when p takes value p_i, and p_i is the least marked value consistent with D. We consider (3) to be a domain-specific learning procedure, comparable to the subset principle in that respect; however, like the markedness condition (2) it possesses greater likelihood of being computationally tractable.

In present terms the markedness condition (2) defines the order in which the parametric choices expressed in the null-subject parameter are explored by the child learner, and (3) the learning principle that can be used to select the correct value of the parameter on the basis of positive-only data, a process that may be termed *positive identification*.

> (4) *Positive identification*
> A parameter value is positively identified just in case all observed positive instances are consistent with that value.

However, learning is in part determined externally by the data presented to the learner, and positive identification can be fully successful only if the data are totally consistent with one of the set of values associated with the parameter, which, we already know, cannot be guaranteed under the parameter. The following consequence immediately ensues: if the correct language is any language other than L(a), the selection of each one might lead to overgeneralization within that language, as shown in the following section.[1]

7.1.2   Exact identification

Suppose that L(b) is the ambient language. Recall that in L(b) all argumental subjects must be overt. Then, when presented with sentences with null nonarguments, the learner is bound to conjecture the parametric identity of the language. But notice that, given the 'no negative evidence' assumption, apparently there is nothing that would prevent him from overgeneralizing *within* the correct language, producing sentences with overt nonarguments, as exemplified here with respect to German.

(5) *Heute sind es zwei Kinder gekommen
'today there came two children'

Now consider that L(c) is the language to be learned. The presence in the data of sentences with both kinds of null nonreferential subjects should be sufficient to rule out L(a) and L(b), pointing to L(c) as the most likely choice. But the learner might still overgeneralize within L(c). That is, the learner might erroneously regard sentences with overt quasi-argument subjects, such as the Yiddish example (6), as well as those with nonargument subjects, to be in L(c).

(6) *Haynt geyt es a regn
'it's raining today'

Likewise in the case of L(d). The appearance in the data of null referential subjects should straightaway rule out L(a), L(b), and L(c). But the problem of possible overgeneralization to overt pleonastics within L(d) is still there. Considering that quite often expletives are homophonous with certain referential pronouns or some other semantically nonempty items (e.g. Yiddish *es* and English *it* have referential counterparts; notably, Welsh *hi* is third person feminine singular), in principle overgeneralization can occur even though overt expletives are totally absent in the language being learned, as they are in Italian.[2] In its weakest form, this type of overgeneralization may simply consist of an expectation on the part of the learner that non-null pleonastic subjects are possible, without any definite knowledge of the particular lexical form(s) they would actually assume.

The upshot is that a learner equipped solely with the parameter as defined in the previous chapter, the markedness condition (2) and the learning procedure (3), may not be guaranteed to be entirely successful. Though absolutely central to the process of parameter fixation, positive identification could well prove to be insufficient, since, owing to the nonexistence of certain predicted structures, the principle (3) will not ensure that the learner's language as defined by the parameter is extensionally identical to the ambient language. To put it more succinctly, (3) may not be able to *exactly identify* the ambient language. Recall that the learning procedure (3) is designed to be driven solely by positive-only evidence. It seems then that although this type of evidence is effective in positively identifying a language from among the four possible ones, it is not effective in exactly identifying that language. Beyond the point in linguistic development when a parameter is fixed, say following the application of the learning procedure (3), the learner might have to employ further inferencing strategies that are essentially data-driven; that is to say, exact identification would require that in relation to the missing forms the learning system must be completely guided by the record of linguistic examples made available to him, rather than exclusively by the specific innate entities modelled in the form of the parameter, and (2), (3) above.

Patently, whatever exact identification may involve, under the present approach it will presuppose positive identification. Further, it will require that the learner should discover the exact extent of difference between the language predicted by the target parameter value and the 'incomplete' ambient language. Suppose that the language defined by the target value (a) of a parameter is L(a), and the corresponding ambient language is L(|a). Then exact identification may be defined in this manner.

(7) *Exact identification*
   A parameter value (a) is exactly identified just in case
   a. it is positively identified; and
   b. the difference between L(a) and L(|a) is known.

Keeping this definition in mind, let us now try to ascertain the mechanisms whereby exact identification can come about.

A solution to the projection problem described in the last section, which could lead to exact identification, would be for the learner to undergeneralize within the conjectured language. This can be accomplished by noticing the nonoccurrence of the relevant types of overt pleonastic subjects in the 'incomplete' data, in other words by resorting to what Chomsky (1981) called indirect negative evidence (Lasnik 1990, Oehrle 1985; also Berwick and Pilato 1987, see below). Chomsky writes that

> a not unreasonable system can be devised with the operative principle that if certain structures or rules fail to be exemplified in relatively simple expressions, where they would be expected to be found, then a (possibly marked) option is selected excluding them in the grammar, so that a kind of 'negative evidence' can be available even without corrections, adverse reactions, etc. There is good reason to believe that direct negative evidence is not necessary for language acquisition, but indirect negative evidence may be relevant. (1981: 8–9)

What this means is that if there are structures that are predicted to exist by the learner's grammar, and that do not appear in the stream of data after *n* positive instances (where n is a sufficiently large number indicating the size at a given time of the ever expanding corpus of data), then the learner is capable of the negative inference that these structures are in fact missing from the ambient language. A more precise framework of this nature is developed in Oehrle (1985), which we take this opportunity to adapt in the following pages.

As Oehrle (1985) suggests, the learning of partially regular morphological or syntactic paradigms can be modelled by means of a set of mathematical functions each of whose arguments is a pair $\langle x, t \rangle$, where x denotes an underived (or 'default') form, and t is a temporal value indicating the number of examples observed. The value of these functions can be either x', a derived (or any possible related) form attested in positive data, or one of the two symbols θ and *. These last two respectively mean mere nonoccurrence and definite non-existence, i.e. θ shows that the form is hitherto unknown to the learner, and * means that the function is undefined at a given argument. Such a function, call it f, represents a pattern possible under a paradigm. It assigns to each $\langle x, t \rangle$ at most one value (or maybe none at all). This involves three noteworthy possibilities.

(a) $f\langle x, t \rangle = x'$
(b) $f\langle x, t \rangle = \theta$
(c) $f\langle x, t \rangle = *$

We shall use Oehrle's (1985) account of the auxiliary verbs in English for the purpose of illustration. The English auxiliary system, which contains several defective paradigms (see Baker 1981), could maximally have forty-eight possible forms distinguished by three persons, two numbers, two tenses, two polarities, and two positions (these last corresponding to declarative or inverted word order). Now let us envisage a function $f = \langle 1,$ sg, pres, neg, dec$\rangle$, and a function $f' = \langle 1,$ sg, pres, neg, inv$\rangle$, and see some of the values they can assign to the stem *be* (in standard English) in the course of acquisition.

(a) $f'\langle be, t \rangle = aren't$
(b) $f\langle be, t \rangle = \theta$
(c) $f\langle be, t \rangle = *$ (*amn't, *ain't)

What concerns us most, obviously, is the conversion of (b) to (c), that is, the negative inference from nonoccurrence to total absence. This is best accomplished by means of a strength function Sf, which associates an integer with each possible form as a measure of how frequently the form in question has been encountered, or has failed to appear, in the evidence.

Apart from other reasons, the use of the strength function is important to deal with 'noisy' data, which might contain a few odd examples of an incorrect pattern. Sf takes as its argument a triple consisting of (a) x, a base form, (b) z, which can be any x' where $f\langle x, t \rangle = x'$ (i.e. any attested non-base form), or θ (i.e. nonoccurrence of any such x'), and (c) a time t at which z has a particular strength s ($=0$ or greater), s being the value of Sf at $\langle x, z, t \rangle$.

$$Sf\langle x, z, t \rangle = s$$

If the attested examples do not acquire a threshold level k of strength, or if the nonoccurrence of such examples does acquire k, by a designated time t^*, the learner, construed as function f, will then be entitled to a negative inference as to the nonexistence of an x' in the ambient language. On the other hand, if a derived form does acquire k by t^*, the learner will decide that that form is in the ambient language. Needless to remark, the conclusions reached at t^* will remain unchanged thereafter. These possibilities may be formally expressed in this manner.

(a) $Sf\langle x, \theta, t^* \rangle = k+ \; (k+ \geqslant k)$
      Therefore: $f\langle x, t^*+ \rangle = {}^* \; (t^*+ \geqslant t^*)$

(b) $Sf\langle x, x', t^* \rangle = k- \; (k- < k)$
      Therefore: $f\langle x, t^*+ \rangle = {}^*$

(c) $Sf\langle x, x', t^* \rangle = k+$
      Therefore: $f\langle x, t^*+ \rangle = x'$

Note that the strength value of k need not be absolute, but can (in fact may have to) be relativized. For example, it can be made dependent on a similar value for a related item y whose frequency of occurrence should have some predictable relationship with the frequency of x. So a level of strength will be considered sufficiently low for x only in comparison with the frequency of y in the data. The motivation behind that would be to prevent the learner from ruling out forms which are just rare, rather than non-existent.

Oehrle (1985) outlines a similar account of the learning of the dative alternation, a syntactic paradigm exhibiting the same mixture of productivity and partial irregularity as the auxiliary system. The logic is that part of the learning process consists of relating *to*-dative constructions to double-NP constructions. In case the latter do not exist, the learner then excludes them on the basis of measurement of strength. It is noteworthy that this account contrasts with other accounts of the phenomenon, which depend either exclusively on positive-only evidence (e.g. Baker 1979, Mazurkewich and White 1984,[3] also cf. Pinker 1989), or on a combination of the direct and indirect use of positive evidence (Randall 1985).

It should not be too hard to see that, assuming our definition of the null-subject parameter to be essentially correct, the problem raised by the parameter belongs to the same class of projection puzzles as the problems related to the dative alternation and the auxiliary system, and that the solution outlined above is in essence equally relevant to the matter in hand. By way of illustration, suppose that the value (b) of the parameter is the value positively identified by the learner, and that the learner incorrectly assumes a configuration type c' containing an overt nonargument to be in L(b), together with c, the null counterpart of c'. Suppose further that the learner notes the nonoccurrence of tokens of c' against a value of k that is relativized to the strength m assigned to c, so that in some precise sense k symbolizes the expected strength of c' in comparison with m (maybe k is fixed at a value considerably less than m, since the use of overt pronouns is pragmatically restricted in null subject languages). The learner may now be considered to exclude c' as follows, where Sf is the relevant strength function, f is a function that can decide whether c' does ($f\langle c, t^*\rangle = c'$) or does not ($f\langle c, t^*\rangle = *$) exist, θ denotes the nonoccurrence of c', and t^* the time taken by the learner to reach the final conclusion.

$$Sf\langle c, \theta, t^*\rangle = k + (k + \geqslant k)$$
Therefore: $f\langle c, t^* + \rangle = * (t^* + \geqslant t^*)$

Since the configuration c' fails to appear in the data by t^*, the learner concludes that f is not defined at $\langle c, t^* + \rangle$, i.e. c' is not in the ambient language. Under our approach, this type of learning, which is designed to ensure exact identification, is considered to come into operation once positive identification has taken place, its task being to bridge any gaps between the predictions made by the parameters of UG and the linguistic data actually exhibited. Whereas positive identification is a simple selective process that can occur on the basis of a small number of triggering instances, exact identification further consists of inferential processes which involve much closer and extensive handling of the data, including the keeping of a record of certain examples.

Clearly, the use of indirect negative inference in a manner akin to that outlined above will indeed be sufficient to exactly identify the correct language from data that are incomplete with respect to the parameter. However, whether this type of evidence is at all necessary for successful acquisition is a question which is not easy to answer, not least because rival evidential strategies are not easy to compare.

7.2   Indirect negative inference: further justifying assumptions

Although the use of implicit negative evidence is logically feasible, it has yet to be fully established if it is psychologically plausible as well. The consensus in the field seems to be that a learnability framework that is susceptible to a variety of evidential strategies, some depending on nonpositive instances, is psychologically unmotivated and therefore untenable. Further, it is possible to argue that indirect negative evidence is not really necessary, since alternative accounts based on positive-only evidence are usually possible.

In relation to the null-subject parameter, one such alternative may be based on the view that there are in fact three different parameters rather than just one, each corresponding to one of the three types of subjects. That is, there would be a separate parameter for nonargument subjects, another one for quasi-argument subjects, and a third one for referential subjects. Armed with these three parameters, the learner would then be in no danger of overgeneralization, as each of them could be set independently on observation of relevant positive evidence. However, there are a number of problems which such an overly conservative solution must instantly face. Firstly, by fragmenting the parameter, it will miss the important generalization that the factor underlying the three new parameters, i.e. the optionality of nominative Case, is the same. Secondly, due to increase in the number of possibilities, it will predict language types that are unattested; for instance, it will predict a language which admits null referential subjects, but does not allow null nonarguments. The second obstacle can apparently be removed by further stipulating dependencies between the parameters, so that referential subjects can be omitted if and only if quasi-arguments and nonarguments are omitted, and quasi-arguments may be omitted just in case null nonarguments are admitted. But it is not obvious whether the resulting set of parameters and dependencies would really be distinct from the single parameter as proposed. Eventually, it might not appear worthwhile to complicate the initial state of the learning system to such an extent only in order to save the 'no negative evidence' assumption.

Another alternative may go like this. Let us presume that the learner intrinsically expects the data to be deficient due to some quasi-linguistic considerations. To put it more concretely, assume that the following constraint, which stipulates the absence of redundant forms such as expletive subjects unless they are observed in positive data, is a part of the learner's *a priori* linguistic baggage. Here 'redundant' means syntactically optional *and* pragmatically useless.

(8) *Redundancy constraint*
Assume redundant forms to be absent unless they are exemplified in positive data.

Supposing that the absence of overt expletives in null-subject languages is the norm, this constraint, comparable but not identical to the Avoid Pronoun Principle, would make it possible for the parameter to be correctly fixed from positive-only evidence. Is the problem really resolved if we assume a constraint like (8) to be a part of the preexisting linguistic and learnability structures? We would like to argue that there are a number of reasons why such a move could be ill-advised; instead, allowing some measure of implicit negative evidence might be a better option.

By itself the constraint in question (or any other similar assumption) is not independently motivated, its only justification being that it salvages the 'no negative evidence' condition. To reiterate a point made before, though ensuring a simple view of evidence, the constraint does not necessarily simplify the learning system, for it will make the initial state more intricate. As a built-in device for undergeneration, it will be in competition with the parameter under consideration whose primary task is to generate well-formed structures. Further, in terms of markedness the constraint appears to be in conflict with the parameter. Whereas the latter defines a language with overt pleonastics, e.g. L(a), to be less marked, the constraint in question implies that, owing to some pragmatically motivated component of Universal Grammar, overt pleonastics are less acceptable than the nonlexical ones. We think there are compelling reasons for postulating that grammatical principles and pragmatic tendencies should never be conflated, since a maximally simple theory will be obtained by excluding pragmatic processes from the characterization of Universal Grammar (see Smith 1988, 1989 for a discussion of how pragmatics could be related to parameter setting).

Another danger in stipulating constraints like (8) is that it is all too easy to go on adding such *ad hoc* devices; the resulting interplay between parameters and constraints is very likely to become too unfettered. Finally, such constraints are in any case mere substitutes for some sort of implicit negative data. So one might as well acknowledge that this kind of evidence is not altogether irrelevant to language acquisition. In short, it seems parsimonious to assume that the parameter is as stated in the previous chapter, and the extensional shortfall in languages is due to pragmatic factors (cf. (8) above), not to be accounted for within a theory of grammar or learnability, though they might have a place in the description of particular grammars. Moreover, it is suggested that some limited use of indirect negative evidence should be considered justifiable in certain cases, largely to enable the learner to eliminate some consequences of a parametric choice.

In principle many writers agree, in keeping with Chomsky's (1981) *obiter dictum*, that a theory incorporating indirect negative evidence is not entirely implausible (e.g. Pinker 1984, Randall 1985, Wexler 1987); thus Wexler remarks that indirect negative evidence 'might potentially be a valuable part of a theory of language learning' (1987: 38). However, in general the idea is regarded with considerable scepticism for a variety of reasons, the more important of which we shall endeavour to scrutinize in the following paragraphs.

A serious drawback can be that indirect negative evidence might also exclude some usually complex structures that are perfectly well formed but probably extremely uncommon, e.g. the fully expanded English auxiliary phrase (Wexler 1987). As mentioned before, in certain cases it might be feasible to relativize the notion of what frequency of occurrence is good enough for a decision to be made in relation to a particular part of grammar, a possibility which we shall not explore further. There is another solution, however, which is directly relevant to the case just mentioned; there is a likelihood that certain aspects of a grammar not figuring directly or prominently in positive data might follow indirectly from its other aspects that are directly and explicitly exemplified, what Randall (1985) calls indirect positive evidence. For some evidence supportive of this possibility we simply refer to a concrete proposal put forward by Berwick and Pilato (1987), which describes a machine induction system that learns some partly regular subparts of English. These authors claim that their system can induce the rare, fully expanded auxiliary sequence of English on the basis of simple, commonly occurring sequences. Simplistically, *could have been being given* is inferrable from examples like *could have been given*, and *have been being given*. Considering that such complex rare forms can possibly be acquired in the complete absence of directly relevant exemplars in the evidence, one could assert that their existence does not necessarily pose a threat to a proposal advocating a limited, well-defined role for indirect negative evidence.

It may be beneficial at this point to expatiate on the structure of the Berwick and Pilato model, as it throws some light on several aspects of the issue under consideration. Berwick and Pilato (1987) describe a machine-learning system that is designed to mimic some properties of human language learning. The system learns two partly regular (in the mathematical sense; see section 3.2.1) subparts of the grammar of English, the auxiliary verb sequence, and the noun phrase specifier system (i.e. the sequence of articles, adjectives, etc., preceding a noun). These authors argue that domain-specific learning mechanisms, that is, parameter fixation and the like, are relatively efficient as far as the learning of complementational patterns (systems of complements under X-bar theory) is concerned, but they are not eminently successful in dealing with more idiosyncratic specifier systems, such as the NP specifier system and the auxiliary sequence (the latter is loosely taken to be the specifier system of VP). For these more powerful (possibly domain-general) inductive techniques may be required, which can be shown to be effective if they work in conjunction with a small hypothesis space as prescribed by a nativist linguistic model. Berwick and Pilato (1987) reason that the 'no learning theory needed' view prevalent in nativist frameworks ignores the complexity of the task of acquisition, as natural-language syntax is not always systematic enough to be learnable from simple positive instances. Consequently, Berwick and Pilato's (1987) system makes auxiliary use of some indirect negative evidence.

The learning device in Berwick and Pilato (1987) is computationally tractable because it is formally restricted, just as the hypothesis space is delimited by a theory of grammar. The device is a k-reversible deterministic finite-state automaton (DFA), where the value of k denotes the power of the inductive inference device, with a 0-reversible automaton representing the simplest kind of word induction. A higher value for k signifies more conservative inference. (An automaton is reversible if all its arcs can be reversed, and the initial state and the final state can be mutually exchanged; see Berwick and Pilato 1987 for further information.) The value of k denotes the length of a *prefix*, that is, a substring prefixed to a string; the rest of the string is termed the *tail*.

When two prefixes in the language being observed have a tail in common, the automaton concludes that the two prefixes can be followed by the same set of tails. Thus, on observing the three-sentence corpus *Mary bakes cakes*, *John bakes cakes*, and *Mary eats pies*, with the prefixes underlined, a 0-reversible automaton would infer a new string, i.e. *John eats pies*, to be in the target language, thus making the language 0-reversible which it can now fully recognize. A higher value for k will require matching of tails of increasingly longer prefixes; for example, 1-reversibility will involve longer prefixes *Mary bakes* and *John bakes*, and the inference of a new string will not be forced, since both these prefixes already have all the tails (*cakes*) in common. But notice that if a fourth sentence *John bakes pies* was added to the corpus, then a new string *Mary bakes pies* would have to be inferred to retain 1-reversibility.

As trivially illustrated above, the system can infer sentences not presented in positive evidence from those that are. The power of the inference system is boosted every time after the observation of the complete set of examples (hence on the basis of implicit negative information) the system fails to correctly learn the target language. Suppose a 0-reversible DFA is implemented first, and the system overgeneralizes, inferring many illegal examples. Once the complete set of data has been observed, the system can then infer that the overgeneral forms it admits are not in the target language, so it will switch on to the more powerful 1-reversible DFA, and so forth, until it has discovered the specific k-reversible DFA which is neither too weak nor too powerful, that is to say, which learns the corpus exactly. As the technical detail does not concern us here, we shall refer the interested reader to the paper cited above.

For the purpose of illustration, we shall use Berwick and Pilato's (1987) account of the learning of the English auxiliary system, which is conceived as a 1-reversible regular language. To be precise, the target language is a corpus of ninety-two declarative statements (in the third person singular) containing as many variants of the English auxiliary sequence. All major auxiliaries, including nine modals, are represented, and tense, aspect, voice and *do*-support are taken into account. According to Berwick and Pilato (1987), the system overgenerates if a 0-reversible DFA is implemented; a 1-reversible 8-state DFA exactly infers the entire corpus of ninety-two examples from only forty-eight examples; a 3-reversible model requires more examples, and a 3 + -reversible model yields no successful inference from any proper subset of the corpus. Note that the NP specifier system, a subsystem of English that is considerably more irregular than the auxiliary system, involves an 81-state 2-reversible DFA, and a corpus of 735 examples, out of which 359 are required for correct inference. Berwick and Pilato (1987) point out that the difficulty of the NP specifier system relative to the auxiliary system is well-attested in the developmental data;

compared with the acquisition of the NP specifier system, children are known to make far fewer errors in the acquisition of the auxiliary system.

Another major objection to the use of implicit negative evidence rests on the assumption that it necessarily requires a 'profligate' learning system, consisting of undesirably rich learning strategies. This may be particularly true with regard to problems involving morphosyntactic overgeneraliz-ations, the English dative alternation being a case in point. Assuming lexical conservatism (Baker 1979), a solution to such problems depending on indirect negative evidence will necessitate keeping the record of the nonoccurrence of structures associated with a large number of verbs on an item-by-item basis, arguably an implausible task as it requires considerable memory resources (Mazurkewich and White 1984, Randall 1985, but cf. Oehrle's 1985 model).

Whatever the merits and demerits of implicit negative evidence in cases of the type mentioned in the last paragraph, it should be obvious that parametric theory offers a highly restrictive view of the *a priori* choice space available to the learner, as each parameter can vary only in a small number of ways. Therefore, it appears psychologically realistic to hypothesize that the child is sensitive to nonoccurrence of certain types of data expected under the preexisting schemas, a hypothesis that would be untenable in a less restrictive linguistic framework. Since parameters associated with a small number of values constitute a very narrow search space, slightly expanding the use of primary evidence (as it is relevant to parameter fixation) to embrace some measure of attention to the nonoccurrence of certain clearly expected data does by no means appear to be a disastrous step – provided, of course, that it is accompanied by appropriate restrictions. Wexler rightly points out that indirect negative evidence can prove to be useful only if the theory of language learning incorporating it is 'a very heavily constrained theory which determines when and how it is used' (1987: 38). In the spirit of this remark, the following constraint on the use of indirect negative evidence, implicit throughout the foregoing discussion, is proposed here.

> (9) On no account can the choice of a parameter value, or a change in the value of a parameter, be made solely on the basis of indirect negative evidence.

What this says is that no amount of indirect negative evidence, in and of itself, can determine the value of a parameter; this type of evidence can only be used in conjunction with (direct) positive evidence. It is the latter which always converges upon a candidate value; indirect negative evidence may then be invoked in the event of the need to exclude some consequences of a choice. Restricting implicit negative evidence is a move designed to ensure a sufficient degree of conservatism in the learning system. To conclude this discussion, it is urged that the type of evidence under discussion should be added to the class of possible solutions to the learnability problems.

The foregoing discussion does not necessarily imply that relatively less restrictive uses of implicit negative evidence are completely forbidden. There is room for speculation as to whether indirect negative evidence can have some further applications. Consider a parameter which yields a subset hierarchy in the extensional sense; e.g. the governing category parameter as formulated by Wexler and Manzini, which ranges over values a, ..., e; moreover, $L(a) \subseteq L(b) \subseteq L(c) \subseteq L(d) \subseteq L(e)$ for anaphors. In that case positive-only evidence should be sufficient to determine learnability. But does that mean that the learner employs indirect negative evidence only when confronted with a parameter like the one controlling the distribution of null subjects?

We speculate that it might be that the learner is indeed more consistent in the use of this kind of evidence than has been hitherto suggested in this chapter, perhaps in the following manner. Suppose the learner selects value (a) of the five-valued governing category parameter on the basis of positive-only evidence; in such cases we say that the parameter has been *positively identified*. Given that inferential exclusion of features not exemplified in the evidence is a learning strategy which is part of the learning system, it is conceivable that, say, after the observation of n data consistent with (a), the learner not only selects (a) but also excludes (e). Likewise, after observation of *2n* data, he excludes (d), and so forth, until all values other than (a) are ruled out. Clearly, the same logic is applicable *vis-à-vis* the values of the null-subject parameter when they fall into subset–superset relations; in particular, we know that $L(c)$ can be a proper subset of $L(d)$. Thus *exact identification* of value (c) may similarly entail exclusion of value (d), turning into what may be termed *strong identification*.

In other words, the predetermined parametric space is searched not just unidirectionally but bidirectionally, somewhat like Mitchell's 'version spaces' model of concept learning (Mitchell 1978, 1983) which uses direct negative instances in place of indirect negative evidence, along with positive instances. Driven by the two types of evidence, the model searches through all the possible versions of a concept located within a partially preordered hypothesis space; the ordering of different versions of a concept is partial because several orderings through the version space are possible. The major strategy is to conjecture two sets of versions of the target concept at a given time, one consisting of versions compatible with all the positive instances received, and the other of versions compatible with the negative instances observed to date. The process continues until both the sets converge on an identical item.

The comparable logic for a parameter fixation model is as follows. Positive and indirect negative data are together employed to search an (absolutely) ordered choice space, leading to the correct identification of a parameter value. Only one value is inferred at any given time in the history of learning (but cf. Valian 1989, 1990). Concomitantly, indirect negative data are counted toward strong identification, i.e. toward exclusion of choices which constantly fail to be exemplified. Note that such bidirectional search is in accordance with the constraint (9) above; indirect negative evidence alone is never used to select a value.

In conventional learnability terms strong identification is not logically necessary. As it stands it is merely an additional epistemological condition on the learner, requiring that at some point in the process of acquisition he stop learning and therefore stop expecting new data. Whether strong identification is empirically desirable is a matter for further research.

7.3 Significance for the current approaches

In this chapter we have proposed a metric for parameter values which regards the range of grammatical categories affected by a value as being criterial for evaluating markedness. It is natural to ask what implications our approach has for the two major current approaches to parameter fixation, i.e. the views incorporated in the work of Wexler and Manzini and that of Hyams, a question we shall try to address in the following pages.

7.3.1 Binding parameters and markedness

As our approach is closely related to that of Wexler and Manzini (1987) and Manzini and Wexler (1987), it would be interesting to consider if it is extendible to the binding parameters as defined by these authors. If so, then that would provide additional support for our contention that markedness is not a function of the application of certain set-theoretical constructs to the languages generated by parameter values.[4]

It is relatively easy to show that the proper antecedent parameter lends itself to a view of markedness compatible with (2) rather straightforwardly. Recall that the parameter has two values, (a) and (b). Under value (a) the set of proper antecedents contains only subjects, and under value (b) the set of proper antecedents includes both subjects and objects. Thus the set of proper antecedents defined by value (b) is a proper superset of the set of proper antecedents defined by value (a), and value (b) includes value (a) exactly as the markedness condition (2) requires.

What about the governing category parameter? We believe that this parameter too is compatible with the present approach. We begin by pointing out a weakness in the formulation of the parameter, which recognizes five different governing categories characterized respectively by the presence of (a) a subject, (b) an Infl, (c) a tense, (d) an indicative tense, and finally (e) a root tense. By way of demonstration we shall focus largely on anaphors, but the argument is intended to apply to pronominals as well. To exemplify the weakness mentioned above, we shall only refer to the Italian anaphor *sè* and the Icelandic anaphor *sig*; it should be clear, though, that, *mutatis mutandis*, the point is equally relevant to all other types of marked anaphors. Under the governing-category parameter the correct definitions of governing category for *sè* and *sig* require the presence of Infl and indicative tense respectively. But consider these pairs of Italian (10) and Icelandic (11) examples (adapted from Manzini and Wexler 1987).

(10)a. Alice$_j$ guardò i [$_{NP}$ ritratti   di sè$_{i/j}$ di Mario$_i$]
     Alice looked at   portraits of Refl of Mario
     'Alice looked at Mario's portraits of Refl'
   b. [$_{NP}$ ritratti di sè$_i$ di Mario$_i$]
     'Mario's portraits of Refl'
(11)a. Jón$_j$ heyrði ($_{NP}$ lysingu   Mariu$_i$ af sér$_{i/j}$]
     Jon heard   description Maria(gen) of Refl
     'Jon heard Maria's description of Refl'
   b. [$_{NP}$ lysingu Mariu$_i$ af sér$_i$]
     'Maria's description of Refl'

According to Wexler and Manzini the reflexives in (10a) and (11a) are not bound in the minimal governing category containing them and their antecedents, i.e. the NP, since it lacks Infl/tense, but in the maximal governing category, i.e. the sentence containing the NP and an Infl/tense. We assume that it is legitimate to speak of the grammaticality of any kind of maximal projections, not just sentences; this would be in keeping with the well-established assumption that grammatical processes are essentially category-neutral, and that the category S has no privileged status in a theory of Universal Grammar. Now, if (10b) and (11b) are also grammatical alongside (10a) and (11a), as we assume they are, then the relevant definitions of the governing categories are inadequate for these constructions, as under their definitions both (10b) and (11b) are wrongly predicted to be ill-formed. Note that in their independent capacity the NPs in (10b) and (11b) do not contain an Infl or a tense, respectively, as required by the governing-category parameter, so they can be grammatical only by virtue of being a part of an S. We have delineated the problem only with respect to NPs, but the logic is equally relevant to small clauses, which, just like NPs, can be governing categories in their own right under no value other than (a). The point we wish to make is that, although there is no way out of this dilemma under the subset condition, a solution is possible precisely in terms of the markedness condition (2).

Suppose that the set of governing categories permitted in UG contains five types corresponding to the five values of the parameter under discussion. For convenience we shall write a governing category with a subject as GC(A), a governing category with an Infl as GC(B), a governing category with a tense as GC(C), a governing category with an indicative tense as GC(D), and a governing category with a root tense as GC(E). One could argue that the parametric variation captured in the governing-category parameter is not to be explained by stipulating a different single governing category related to each value, but by a gradual increase in the number of governing categories allowed by the marked values. Thus, value (a) permits only one type of governing category, which is GC(A). On the other hand under value (b) both GC(A) and GC(B) are legitimate governing categories, and so forth. The governing categories so permitted under each of the five values are listed in (12).

(12)a. GC(A)
    b. GC(A), GC(B)
    c. GC(A), GC(B), GC(C)
    d. GC(A), GC(B), GC(C), GC(D)
    e. GC(A), GC(B), GC(C), GC(D), GC(E)

This would require a slight revision in the statement of the parameter, but the result would be in accord with the definition of markedness in (2). If such a revision is justified, then one would be able to say that the reflexives in the examples in (10) and (11) are, or may be, bound within NPs, i.e. within their minimal governing categories. We can now define a minimal governing category for anaphors as in (13a), and that for pronominals as in (13b).

(13) *Minimal governing category*
   a. γ is a minimal governing category for α, α an anaphor, if it is the minimal maximal projection containing α and its antecedent.
   b. γ is a minimal governing category for α, α a pronominal, if it is the minimal maximal projection containing α and the antecedents from which α is free.

We thus hold that an anaphor is always bound, and a pronominal is always free, within its minimal governing category. In sum, we believe that this revised view of the binding parameters is preferable, and that it lends support to the notion of markedness already shown to be relevant to the null-subject parameter.

7.3.2   Developmental implications

We now turn to a reappraisal of the other major viewpoint, namely Hyams's developmental approach (1986, and elsewhere). The parameter, as viewed in the present context, encapsulates the way the knowledge of the null-subject phenomenon could be determined from primary linguistic evidence, without necessarily making clear predictions regarding the course of acquisition. In general we do not regard a learnability theory as being a theory of development. Nevertheless, such predictions as can be deduced from it are as follows. In the simplest case each value of the parameter can be fixed straightaway, provided the relevant evidence is available. In the more complicated situations, limited to the learning of the marked values, there is a possibility that one or more values which are less marked than the correct one could be provisionally chosen first. However, it is not predicted that any provisional choices will necessarily be apparent in the form of temporal stages of acquisition, as such choices, if made at all, may not last long enough to impinge on the production data. Similarly, considering that early child grammars do not license expletive subjects (Hyams 1986, Radford 1990), which anyway are functionally redundant, and that these grammars allow even thematic subjects to be null, we do not expect the effect of the possible overgeneralization to overt pleonastics to be manifestly reflected in child language data.

This is in contrast with the approach advocated by Hyams, which rests on the claim that not only can provisional wrong choices be made, but that in some cases they must be made. For example, Hyams contends that the null-subject parameter is first fixed at the null value regardless of the nature of the language being learned. Thus children learning languages as diverse as Italian, German, and English are supposed to start out with the assumption that the language they are learning is null subject, and they stay with this assumption for quite some time until restructuring, for whatever reason, occurs. More importantly from the present point of view, Hyams's (1986) account depends crucially on the assumption that the parameter yields (partially) intersecting languages, so that crucial triggers (sentences containing pleonastic subjects in the case of non-pro-drop languages, and sentences without overt referential subjects in the case of pro-drop languages) are always available. However, as far as our version of the parameter is concerned, among language types predicted by it there is at least one instance of proper inclusion, i.e. between L(c) and L(d), that is bound to create an insurmountable subset problem (Manzini and Wexler 1987) if, in keeping with the spirit of Hyams's analysis, L(d) is considered to be the initial choice by the child. We, therefore, conclude that, to the extent that our view of the parameterization of null subjects is a correct model of the cross-linguistic variation, Hyams's (1986) view is indefensible on learnability-theoretic grounds.

In recent work Hyams has revised her earlier analysis of the null-subject parameter and its setting (Hyams 1987). The move is motivated by certain inadequacies of the hypothesis that in null-subject languages Agr = PRO (see Guilfoyle 1984, Hyams 1987, Lebeaux 1987 for a discussion; also see chapter 5). For example, the previous analysis did not capture the fact that in the acquisition of non-null-subject languages lexical subjects and inflections for tense, etc., appear roughly at the same time. It also failed to take into account the absence of inflections in early null-subject English, although early Italian, though similar in respect of the setting of the null-subject parameter, is known to have inflected paradigms. This would imply that in early Italian, but not in early English, identification of features of the null subject is possible through overt agreement markings.

The current version adopts a new linguistic analysis based on the hypothesis regarding morphological uniformity (Jaeggli and Hyams 1988, Jaeggli and Safir 1989a), which was discussed in the last chapter. Nonetheless, her basic claim regarding acquisition is the same: the null-subject option is preferred over the non-null-subject option. The former now corresponds to the hypothesis on the part of the child that the language to be learned is characterized by morphologically uniform paradigms, that is to say, is either like Italian or like Chinese. If the ambient language is a language like Italian, then positive data readily confirm the initial option. If, on the other hand, the ambient language has a non-uniform inflectional system, as English, then also the child first assumes that the language is morphologically uniform, but in the sense of Chinese rather than Italian; recall that under the Agr = PRO hypothesis early English was considered to be like Italian, not like Chinese! Early English is supposed to be like Chinese also in respect of the identification mechanism involved, which is now considered to be the binding of a subject *pro* by a null topic, following Huang's (1984) analysis of Chinese, with the obvious difference that a variable is not admitted in the subject position. According to Hyams the new analysis is supported by the fact that in the acquisition of richly and uniformly inflected languages like Italian, Polish and Japanese the inflections are acquired quite early, in contrast with the rather late acquisition of inflections in the case of morphologically poor and non-uniform languages (e.g. English). Since in these latter the lexical subjects and morphological markings emerge almost concurrently, suggesting a possible connection, it is proposed that when the child discovers that English is morphologically non-uniform, he automatically infers that null subjects are not available in this language.[5] We decline to comment further on this revised account until further research succeeds in establishing an explicit causal link between inflectional uniformity and the availability of null subjects.

Whatever version of Hyams's approach is adopted, the problem remains that there is no explanation for the supposition that the null choice must initially be made in all cases, although when the ambient language is a non-null-subject language the evidence confirming this fact, whether overt expletives or inflections, is always available to the learner. Even if we suppose that the parameter is indeed binary valued, and that it does not conform to the subset condition, then, as long as there is a good explanation for why early speech tends to lack overt subjects, such as the one offered by Radford (1990), there is no conceivable reason to claim that one choice or the other is made first, as in principle both choices should be equally accessible.

7.4   Towards greater empirical plausibility

Learnability theory has come a long way from its formal origins (e.g. Gold 1967). No doubt formal, logical considerations will, and should, continue to play a major role in argumentation in learnability theory. However, compared with the advances linguistic theory has made towards achieving greater empirical plausibility, it appears that learnability theory has not done much to belie its purely formal origins. The attempt to describe the languages generated under different values of a parameter in terms of simple set-theoretical relations clearly reflects the dominant role mere formal elegance plays in the field. We have strived to argue that the relationship between parameter values and the languages they generate is far from a straightforward one. Consequently, it may be unwise to define markedness merely on the basis of extensional criteria. We have also argued that indirect negative evidence might have an auxiliary but well-defined role in acquisition. We need to realize that in determining learnability logical plausibility alone is not sufficient; it must be shown that the logical assumptions and conclusions are also empirically plausible.

In particular, the fixation of the null-subject parameter has been shown not to be strictly compatible with the subset principle. A slightly less conservative alternative is proposed, which is nevertheless conservative enough to ensure correct learning. The learning seems to encompass not just positive identification, but also exact identification, requiring some indirect negative evidence. The logic is that sometimes, due to pragmatic/quasi-linguistic factors, the languages generated by parameter values may lack a (somewhat marginal) set of constructions which, had they existed, would be perfectly well formed. Therefore, the learner has to notice their nonpresentation in the available data.

Clearly, an unconstrained use of indirect negative evidence will be disastrous to any learnability argument. Hence the restriction that it can only be employed to eliminate a subpart of a choice, but not to identify a value, unless in collaboration with positive data. Positive data are still considered to be the core of the primary data, with indirect negative evidence having an essential but supplementary role, and direct negative evidence remaining irrelevant to the process of acquisition. Overall, indirect negative evidence is feasible only in a language acquisition system in which the hypothesis space available to the learner is dramatically restricted, as in the parameter setting model. Therefore, in the end, the proposal outlined in this chapter is empirically plausible only to the extent that the theory of principles and parameters is empirically plausible.

8 *Review and integration*

It seems that the parameter-setting model has considerable explanatory potential, but that a convergence of a linguistic perspective on learnability, such as the one inherent in parametric theory, and the more formal approaches to language learning, would considerably benefit both these fields. Thus the present study, which represents a contribution to the linguistic investigation of learnability, relies significantly on certain parallels with formal models. With respect to parameter fixation, two apparently contradictory conclusions are in order.

Firstly, it would appear that parameter fixation is not as simple a process as has been claimed. It is clear that the 'no learning theory' hypothesis (e.g. Chomsky 1981, 1986a, Hyams 1986) is far from obviously correct, and that the postulation of at least a domain-specific learning theory is essential (Manzini and Wexler 1987, Wexler and Manzini 1987). The parameter-setting model may embody a relatively simple view of language learning, but this view entails potentially very complex consequences, which are very poorly understood at present.

Secondly, complex though it might be in the sense stated above, the model may turn out to be rather trivial in relation to the complexity of the task required of it. A major achievement of the parametric model is that it is capable of explaining the basic variability of the class of possible grammatical systems directly in terms of the process of acquisition. So it affords a perspective on cross-linguistic diversity that is unifiable with a method of acquiring each member of the class of grammars by using the same set of learning mechanisms. However, it does not offer ready solutions to a number of projection puzzles related to the induction of individual languages. Parametric accounts of variation are very useful insofar as the predicted variation appears to be correct, and the languages associated with parameter values are totally consistent with their respective values. Problems immediately arise if a certain degree of irregularity is present in a linguistic system; such a situation usually foreshadows serious acquisitional difficulties, whose resolution might additionally require some nonparametric inductive learning mechanisms.

Two specific proposals concerning parameter setting were discussed and analysed: the set-theoretical approach (Manzini and Wexler 1987, and Wexler and Manzini 1987), and the developmental approach (Hyams 1986). Both these approaches have one property in common; they assume that no choice available to the learner at any given point in language acquisition is outside the bounds defined by Universal Grammar. Thus under the set-theoretical approach the learnability mechanisms, and under Hyams's analysis the developmental mechanisms, are constrained by linguistic theory. The area of overlap between these approaches may increase considerably if the learnability mechanisms are interpreted developmentally, and *vice versa*. Perhaps neither linguistic theory nor learnability theory should be substituted for a theory of language maturation and development, but undoubtedly the learnability-theoretic argumentation can play an important role in mediating between linguistic and developmental theories. However, the major task of learnability theory is to provide a method of evaluation of a class of grammatical systems in terms of how feasible it would be for the child language learner to acquire them under a given set of circumstances, an aim which, at least insofar as parameter fixation is concerned, might appear to be attainable more naturally without much reference to real-time acquisition (Cinque 1989). Whereas linguistic theory provides a reasonably accurate characterization of the class of natural languages, learnability theory strives to develop precise notions of the learning procedures employed by the learner, the evidence available to him, and the manner in which the evidence and the learner could interact in the acquisitional process.

In our investigation of the null-subject phenomenon we have presented a graded four-valued formulation of the null-subject parameter, in line with Wexler and Manzini's cross-linguistic analysis of the binding phenomena, but we have argued that the subset condition of Wexler and Manzini can be replaced with a more grammatical procedure of the evaluation of markedness of parameter values, a procedure which is also extendible to the binding parameters formulated by these authors. We have further demonstrated that a deterministic view of parameter fixation is not really necessary, provided we are willing to admit a certain degree of inferential learning over and above parameter fixation. One way this could happen is if there is a mismatch between parameter values and the languages they generate, as is the case under our analysis of the null-subject parameter. In such cases some auxiliary role for negative inference from nonoccurring data, i.e. for indirect or implicit negative evidence, appears to us to be a perfectly reasonable assumption. Another possibility to be explored is the extent to which positive evidence is used indirectly, in other words, the learning of certain facts from positive-only evidence helps determine some other related facts in the grammar.

The question of the lack of a total mapping between parameter values and the corresponding languages should be of interest for linguistic theory as well. It is well known that languages possess properties that are sometimes less than systematic. This can be attributed to several factors: fundamental variation at the lexical level with rather idiosyncratic repercussions in the syntax, random or systematic interference from nonlinguistic cognitive modules (e.g. processing, pragmatics), historical evolution of the language, or even the presence of purely fortuitous gaps in languages. In view of all these it seems plausible that the link between languages and parameters may sometimes be slightly inconsistent, resulting in gaps in the data available to the child.

There is of course another reason why a gulf could intervene between languages and parameters; parameters interact, with each choice having deductive consequences in relation to other choices. The standard position in linguistic theory is to try to specify these deductive links implicationally, so that many properties of a grammar are supposed to follow just in case a decision to adopt a particular value of a particular parameter is made. Thus, if a language is pro-drop, it should also have subject inversion, the *that*-trace effect, and so forth, a set of assumptions we consider to be questionable. It appears that often a strong correlation between different grammatical properties may be very difficult to establish cross-linguistically; further, it is possible that some such correlations are probabilistic, rather than deterministic, language-particular, rather than explainable in a unified fashion. This could mean that linguistic theory might have to slightly revise its current agenda which usually aims, we suggest unrealistically, at exhaustive description of cross-linguistic phenomena purely in terms of parametric differences. There is also some need to clearly distinguish language-particular facts from universal principles, so that theoretical extrapolation from one language to another is carried out on a more restrictive basis.

The foregoing overview summarizes some conclusions reached in the course of the present study, but we are under no illusion that these conclusions are anything but provisional. In the following paragraphs some unresolved issues relating to the present study are briefly outlined.

A full-fledged theory of parameter fixation may not be possible until some way is found to describe how parameters interact. Admittedly, we have not offered any concrete suggestions in this regard. Here again fundamental descriptive research will have to make a major contribution.

Not surprisingly, our analysis of the null-subject phenomenon and its learnability raises more questions than it answers. A much wider and more systematic study will be required before any definite answers can be given. The distinction between visibility in LF and PF needs to be investigated further. Also, the licensing and interpretation of *pro* and PRO will have to be considered more extensively than we have been able to do in this book. Regarding pleonastics, we have said virtually nothing about the fact that many languages have two lexical pleonastics (e.g. *it* and *there* in English) with different uses, perhaps consequent upon the definiteness effect (Safir 1985), nor about how the child learns to distinguish the differences between the two. It is not obvious whether the split in the usage of the two types springs from purely language-particular factors, or whether it is governed by some principles of UG (see Travis 1984 for some important discussion). Furthermore, it will be interesting to extensively compare and contrast the distribution of null objects with that of null subjects, and to attempt a unified cross-linguistic theory of null arguments.

The learning theory we have proposed contains several assumptions that will have to be spelled out in greater detail. The relationship between various types of evidence and different learning strategies certainly deserves to be probed in considerable depth. Moreover, it will be highly desirable to empirically investigate the psychological plausibility of the use of implicit negative evidence. In sum, we do hope to have uncovered a number of new questions, or, at least, to have sharpened the issues involved.

Notes

1   The problem of language learnability

1 Note that for the present purposes 'learning' and 'learnable' are neutral terms used to denote all types of changes – whether resulting from maturational mechanisms, domain-specific selective procedures such as parameter setting, or relatively general-purpose learning strategies – which affect the cognitive make-up of the learner due to a combination of internal and external factors. Wexler's following remarks are relevant here.

> At least two senses of *learnable* have been used, and I intend only one of them. One sense is that in which *learnable* means learnable by some simple, general learning mechanism, a mechanism sufficient to account for the learning of any kind of human cognitive capacity. In this sense, *learnable* contrasts with *innate*. It is possible that very little that is characteristic and fundamental in human cognition is learnable in this sense, and it is not this sense which I intend.
>
> The second sense, the one which I *do* intend, is that *learnable* means 'can be learned' (according to some criterion). In other words, an ability (e.g., the ability to speak a natural language) is learnable if there is an (empirically true) way in which the ability can develop. In this sense, if an ability is innate it is learnable (with a perhaps trivial 'learning' component). If the ability develops via a learning mechanism based on other innate capacities, the ability is also learnable (with a less trivial component). In short, any human capacity is learnable. (1982: 295–6)

Also see Osherson and Weinstein (1984a: 275, n 1) for further qualifying remarks in much the same vein.

2 It is generally acknowledged, implicitly or explicitly, that a theory of any part of cognition must at least involve (a) a representational component and (b) a procedural component. Standardly, (a) contains a characterization, such as a theory of grammar, of the mature cognitive system, while (b) specifies a set of procedures connected to a computational aspect of the system, for instance learning and use.

3 This and all subsequent undated references are to both Wexler and Manzini (1987) and Manzini and Wexler (1987).

4 In recent work Chomsky (1986a) has distinguished two notions of language, one relating to the internalized knowledge of language, which he terms I-language; and the other pertaining to language as an externalized phenomenon, called E-language. Chomsky maintains that it is I-language that is of primary empirical interest, not E-language, which is a derivative phenomenon. The term

140

'grammar', in the ordinary sense, is taken by Chomsky (1986a) to refer to a theory of a particular I-language, in contrast with UG which is a theory of innate constraints on I-language in general. How are particular I-languages accounted for in a universalist framework? The answer, obviously, is that some aspects of UG are parameterized, permitting limited variation. The task of a theory of UG, therefore, is twofold: it must specify the universal principles of I-language, and it must also define parameters within which the possibilities of variation are located, thus explaining the existence of particular I-languages.

5 Pullum (1983) argues that the finiteness hypothesis, if at all correct, is uninteresting. For one thing, 'finite' is a very deceptive concept which could actually involve astronomically large magnitudes, for instance the total number of subatomic particles in the universe, so in such cases being finite may practically be nearly as problematic as being infinite. For another, a finite-cardinality class containing a very small number of languages may not be learnable if it is not recognizable or parsable in the first place; on the other hand, given sufficiently realistic constraints, even an infinite class of languages could turn out to be both parsable and learnable; cf. Wexler (1981): on somewhat different grounds Wexler argues that, although the finiteness hypothesis is probably correct, 'finiteness of the class of grammars is not sufficient to guarantee learnability in the appropriate sense' (1981: 46).

6 In McCawley's (1983) view there appear to be sufficient reasons to believe that some general-purpose and language-specific mechanisms interact in the acquisition of a first language. This is not improbable because a first language develops in conjunction with several other cognitive systems, most of which conceptually overlap with language and, beside other things, share a common perceptual input system with the latter. Given the common ground, it is inconceivable that the development of linguistic and non-linguistic systems would be totally disjoint. Therefore the null hypothesis, McCawley asserts, is that general learning mechanisms participate in the acquisition of language in some sense; the onus of disproof is on those who argue otherwise. On metatheoretical grounds it seems parsimonious to posit common learning mechanisms that help develop various specific systems like language. Possibly there is a 'division of labour' between the language-specific principles and the general learning principles, the latter serving the former's purpose during acquisition. On the whole it seems that, considering the successive choice of parameters involved and the highly deductive structure of the theory, the role of learning (of whatever kind) in the parameter-setting model of language acquisition cannot be insignificant (cf. Atkinson 1987).

7 We are concerned with combining a consistent theory of language with a somewhat expanded view of domain-specific learning. Adopting a relatively unconstrained linguistic theory and a correspondingly open-ended approach to acquisition will yield learning mechanisms of the kind proposed by Slobin (1985), which he considers to be part of the human language-*making* capacity.

8 We note here that other contemporary syntactic theories, such as Lexical–Functional Grammar or LFG (Bresnan 1982) and Generalized Phrase Structure Grammar or GPSG (Gazdar et al. 1985), may also be viewed as

candidate theories of UG. Gazdar et al., however, are reluctant to speculate on issues of psychological import, because they feel that it is premature to raise them. For book-length introductory accounts of GB, see Cook (1988), Lasnik and Uriagereka (1988), Radford (1988b), and van Riemsdijk and Williams (1986). Joint introductions to all the three theories – i.e. LFG, GPSG and GB – are contained in Horrocks (1987) and Sells (1985).

2   The components of the linguistic system

1 According to Rothstein 'a predicate is an open one-place syntactic function requiring SATURATION, or closure by an argument' (1983:7). She proposes the following *Rule of Predicate Linking* which is a well-formedness constraint on the distribution of nonargument or predicative XPs, comparable with the θ-criterion, which is a well-formedness condition on argument XPs.

(1)   *Rule of Predicate Linking*
Every non-theta-marked XP must be linked at S-structure to an argument which it immediately c-commands and which immediately c-commands it.

These parallel definitions of predicate (2) and subject (3) follow immediately from (1).

(2)   X is predicated of Y (is a predicate of Y) if and only if X is linked to Y under (1).
(3)   X is the subject of Y if and only if Y is linked to X under (1).

2 It has been noted (e.g. Saleemi 1987) that even an 'external' lexicon, i.e. a dictionary in the conventional sense, when containing extensive grammatical specifications of words, comes very close to being a virtual grammar.

3 Some chain-like sequences are created by a type of linking involving Case transfer, rather than movement, an example being the expletive-argument pairs like (*there, a man*) in this example (cf. Chomsky 1986a).

There is *a man* at the door

These are headed by a Case-marked element (*there*) and terminate in a θ-marked element (*a man*), much like proper A-chains created by movement to acquire Case.

4 A different analysis of the separation of T(ense) and Agr(eement) appears in Beukema and Coopmans (1989), who in their treatment of English imperatives argue that only T is located in I, and that Agr actually originates in C. Further, see Kornai and Pullum (1990) for a critical view of such overelaborate versions of the subtheory in question as presented in Chomsky (1989) and Pollock (1989).

5 Perhaps one concrete manifestation of simplicity is the locality of syntactic operations (Culicover and Wilkins 1984, Koster 1978, 1987); an operation that occurs in a structurally local domain is considered to be less marked, being a core UG operation, compared with a nonlocal one, which is defined over a larger structural domain, and is therefore considered to belong to the marked periphery of UG. Under some analyses UG is viewed as possessing an invariant core (Koster 1987), containing principles and perhaps the least marked (preset) values of parameters; these principles are defined in relation to the smallest domains, which get extended as a result of further parameterization in the

variant core. The periphery is essentially a consequence of the relaxation of certain core constraints. Koster offers a theory of domains and dynasties: under this theory extended domains form *dynasties*, a dynasty being 'a chain of governors such that each governor (except the last one) governs the minimal domain containing the next governor' (1987: 19). A formulation of UG parameters (most of them, anyway) in terms of some notion of locality is potentially significant for learnability from positive evidence. In particular, a theory of parameters organized along these lines appears to be relatable to the theory of conservative parameter fixation built around the subset principle (Berwick 1985, Manzini and Wexler 1987, Wexler and Manzini 1987, also see Koster 1987: 318ff). The reader is referred to chapters 4 and 5 for further related discussion.

We take this opportunity to remind the reader that the term 'markedness' is used in the literature to refer to a number of distinct (though often related) constructs. In particular, what is marked or peripheral for UG may well be part of the core grammar of a particular language, and *vice versa*.

6 German and Insular Scandinavian languages (i.e. Icelandic and Faroese) allow expletive pro-drop, but they do not contain any constructions characterized by anything comparable to free inversion of nominative subjects. (I am thankful to Ken Safir for his very helpful remarks on the question of subject inversion and pro-drop.)

Also notable is the fact that in English and French, both non-null-subject languages, subject inversion is possible with ergative verbs and indefinite NPs, but obviously null subjects are not licensed in the constructions in question.

Some other alleged characteristics of pro-drop languages also do not seem to be inseparable from the pro-drop property. Leaving a discussion of the correlation between rich inflection and pro-drop for chapter 6, we can take the case of long Wh-movement; Russian, which is both pro-drop and subject inverting, does not have such movement, nor indeed any Wh-movement out of finite clauses (Kilby 1987). This suggests that many of the cluster of properties which are supposed to follow from the pro-drop property might in fact follow from more or less independent factors, in some cases, arguably, from independent parameters.

3   The components of the learning system

1 Note that requiring an acquisition theory to explain the course of development is comparable to meeting Pinker's (1979) *developmental condition*.

Pinker (1979) imposes six conditions which any viable theory of language acquisition must strive to fulfil: (a) *the Learnability Condition*, which demands an explanation of the fundamental fact that language can universally be learned by children; (b) *the Equipotentiality Condition*, which requires that a theory should be able to account for the acquisition of any natural language; (c) *the Time Condition*, which says that a theory must assume a natural time scale of acquisition by children; (d) *the Input Condition*, which is concerned with empirically constraining the assumptions about the information available to the child; (e) *the Developmental Condition*, demanding consistency between theoretical predictions and actual developmental phenomena; and (f) *the Cognitive Condition*, which requires compatibility with what is known about children's processing abilities, e.g. attention span, memory limitations, perceptual mechanisms, etc., which are involved in the process of language learning. (Also see Atkinson 1982 for a similar but not identical set of conditions.)

2 Wexler (1989) distinguishes between two types of maturation: UG-constrained maturation and unconstrained maturation. He points out that Felix's (1987) proposal is an example of the latter, which is less desirable than the former. On his view UG-constrained maturation is preferable since it constitutes 'the most restrictive theory which can be empirically maintained at the moment (accounting not only for learnability but for the precise and rich patterns of developmental timing)'; on the other hand, the continuity hypothesis is too restrictive to be compatible with the patterns of development.

  UG-constrained maturation, Wexler explains, allows child grammars which are incorrect with respect to the ambient language, but not ones illicit with respect to the principles of UG. Thus A-chains, when they do appear in child language, cannot fail to obey the UG principles of government and the θ-criterion. This approach suggests that the semantic stage argued for by Felix does not exist, and that maturation occurs throughout development in terms of syntactic change, usually from less to more complex structures.

3 But see Pinker, Lebeaux, and Frost (1987), who contend that Borer and Wexler's (1987) claim is questionable on empirical grounds.

4 It may be useful to point out that, in spite of considerable overlap, 'there are some differences in emphasis' between learning from positive examples and inductive inference (Angluin and Smith 1983: 238).

5 An extensive introduction to the field is provided in Pinker (1979); Atkinson (1982, 1986, 1987) evaluates some more recent developments.

6 See Cohen (1986), Grishman (1986), Hopcroft and Ullman (1979), Levelt (1974, vol. 1), Partee (1978), or Wall (1972), for further detail.

7 To avert any misunderstanding, it is important to point out that the term 'identification' is used differently in linguistic and learnability theories: in the former it is employed to refer to the recovery of the ϕ-features and R-index of an EC, whereas in the latter it means successful learning of an entity. As the reader is bound to notice, suitably contextualized, both senses of the expression are intended in this book.

8 Berwick and Weinberg (1984) contend that considerations following from the theory of computational complexity should take precedence over the classical questions of generative capacity.

9 The accompanying peer commentary provides a critical evaluation of Lightfoot's (1989) version of the degree-0 thesis.

10 Nontechnical introductions to this body of work are provided in Osherson and Weinstein (1984a, 1984b).

11 Recall that the set of surface sentences enumerated by a grammar constitutes its *weak generative capacity*, and the set of structural descriptions specified embodies its *strong generative capacity*. Two grammars are *weakly equivalent* if they generate the same set of sentences, *strongly equivalent* if they generate the

same set of structural descriptions. In the Osherson et al. framework the learner, construed as a learning function, is not required to converge on (= identify) the same grammar of a language L for all texts (sets of data) drawn from L.

4   Approaches to parameter fixation

1 The notion of language being employed here is a restrictive and simplified one, and essentially denotes what may be referred to as a *representative* set of sentences which a single parameter may generate; obviously, to a large extent it abstracts away from the unrestrained operation of recursive processes such as embedding, coordination, and also from the little understood consequences of the interaction of several parameters.

2 Although our discussion here is couched in parametric terms, the underlying logic is as much relevant to any other type of grammatical variation that yields subset relations in the same manner. Most well-known cases of nonparametric overgeneralization are morphosyntactic, e.g. that associated with the dative alternation.

3 Berwick's (1985) conceptualization of the subset principle is different from Wexler and Manzini's in two respects. Firstly, it has an explicit noninstantaneous dimension. Secondly, under his approach the principle emerges as a general learning principle, applicable in linguistic and nonlinguistic (e.g. conceptual system) domains alike (especially see Berwick 1986).

4 Unless otherwise indicated, Wexler and Manzini (1987) and Manzini and Wexler (1987) are the sources of most of the examples that follow.

5 This definition is a compromise between the definitions in Wexler and Manzini (1987) and Manzini and Wexler (1987). The formulation of the parameter in Manzini and Wexler (1987), reproduced below, is more complex. Here 'referential' tense denotes the self-contained tense of an indicative clause, as opposed to the 'anaphoric' tense of a subjunctive clause which is dependent on the tense of the matrix indicative clause.

The Governing Category Parameter

γ is a governing category for α iff γ is the minimal category that contains α and a governor for α and

a. can have a subject or, for α anaphoric, has a subject β, $\beta \neq \alpha$; or

b. has an Infl; or

c. has a Tense; or

d. has 'referential' Tense; or

e. has a 'root' Tense;

if, for α anaphoric, the subject β', $\beta' \neq \alpha$, of γ, and of every category dominating α and not γ, is accessible to α.

The accessibility clause at the end is required (i) to ensure that the i-within-i condition is observed by anaphors (traditionally accessibility is applied to pronouns as well as anaphors; for example, see Chomsky 1981; however, Manzini and Wexler 1987 adopt the view that accessibility is confined to anaphors), and (ii) to exclude from the purview of the parameter certain marked configurations in which anaphors can be coindexed by non-c-commanding antecedents. In such cases the anaphors can corefer freely as they lack accessible antecedents, and therefore are supposed not to have a governing category at all (see Manzini and Wexler 1987 for detail; cf. Manzini 1983; also see Bouchard 1984 for similar views, who maintains that anaphors coindexed with a non-c-commanding antecedent are actually 'false anaphors').

6 That governing categories are indeed parameterized in the manner suggested by Wexler and Manzini and others is of course open to debate; Hyams and Sigurjónsdóttir (1990), for instance, reject this view of parameterization and claim that many of the so-called long-distance anaphors, in particular the Icelandic *sig*, are actually bound variables that can undergo cyclic movement from Infl to Infl in LF. Cole, Hermon and Sung (1990) also seek to analyse the apparently unbounded reflexive binding as consisting of a series of local dependencies.

7 It is difficult to fail to notice the remarkable similarity between a subset hierarchy and the noun phrase accessibility hierarchy (Keenan and Comrie 1977), as both lead to nesting languages.

8 The formal definitions that appear in this chapter, all taken from Manzini and Wexler (1987), are simplified to a single parameter. The reader is referred to Manzini and Wexler (1987) for generalized definitions taking into account the many-parameter cases (also see Manzini and Wexler 1987: 435, n 12, for a further qualification).

9 In a footnote Manzini and Wexler (1987: 433, n 11) point out that there might be more than two parameters in binding theory, e.g. yet another one related to accessibility (cf. Yang 1984). They claim that this parameter will likewise follow the subset condition, since a language for an anaphor which is not associated with an accessibility condition can be demonstrated to be a subset of a language containing an anaphor associated with accessibility.

10 The default assumption is that empty categories are not parameterized, i.e. are invariably characterized by the unmarked value of a parameter, as evidence to the contrary cannot be available to the child (Manzini and Wexler 1987).

11 Further linguistic motivation for Hyams's (1986) account comes from its ability to explain some other phenomena claimed by Hyams to be characteristic of pro-drop languages, in particular Italian, e.g.:

    a. Control into embedded tensed clauses: this is made possible since Infl contains PRO, which can be controlled under standard assumptions
    b. Arbitrary reference associated with the subject of a tensed clause: this proceeds from the assumption that uncontrolled PRO may have arbitrary reference

12 Smith (1988) is critical of the involvement of an essentially pragmatic principle like the Avoid Pronoun Principle in parameter setting, which must be a self-contained syntactic process. The view taken in Smith (1989) is somewhat different.

13 With respect to the subject-inversion parameter, the initial value, according to Hyams, is that pertaining to the absence of inversion (as in English). As a result native English-speaking children never reach a stage where postverbal subjects are permissible. Hyams (1986) is not very explicit as to the implication of this for Italian child language development. She states that Italian children start

producing postverbal subjects quite early, and that it is very difficult to determine if and when they go through a stage characterized by the initial value of the parameter, one major confounding factor being the frequent absence of subjects in the early stages of acquisition.

14 As pointed out in the next chapter, the concept of inter-level isomorphism does not seem very useful in the context of pro-drop. However, it might be relevant to some other cases, for example, various movement rules; see Hyams (1986) for some remarks to this effect.

5 The scope and limits of the current approaches

1 We are not implying that, as it stands, core grammar is a well-defined notion. The assumption, hopefully well founded, is that, as the theory progresses, it should be possible to define this notion with sufficient precision.

2 Koster (1987) suggests that the least marked value of the governing-category parameter is a sixth one, which also falls in with the other five values in relation to the subset condition. This value accounts for anaphors that must be bound in the absolutely minimal category that contains a governor, with no opacity factors involved. So, unlike English *himself*, French *se* cannot be bound across a PP boundary, since PP is the governing category for it, within which no antecedent can be available. Look at these two configurations, where α = anaphor, β = antecedent.

a. $[_s \ldots \beta \ldots [_{PP} \ldots \alpha \ldots]]$
b. $[_s \ldots \beta \ldots \quad \alpha \ldots]$

Configuration (b) is legitimate in both English and French. However, (a) is legitimate in English, but not in French (with respect to *se*). Therefore French is a subset of English in the relevant sense. The following examples (drawn from Koster 1987) should further clarify the point.

a. *Il$_i$ parle [$_{PP}$ de   se$_i$]
   He talks   about Refl
b. Il$_i$ se$_i$ slave
   He Refl washes
c. Il$_i$ parle [$_{PP}$ de   lui-même$_i$]
   He talks   about Refl

3 Manzini and Wexler (1987) suggest that 'definite descriptions or demonstratives' (sometimes referred to as 'anaphoric epithets') can be regarded as being pronominals associated with the unmarked values of both binding parameters; see the use of the epithet *that idiot* in these examples.

a. After they criticized John$_i$, that idiot$_i$ left
b. *They told John$_i$ that that idiot$_i$ shouldn't leave

(a) is grammatical since *that idiot* is not bound; its antecedent does not c-command it. On the other hand, (b) is ill-formed because *that idiot* is bound by *John*. However, it has been claimed that so-called anaphoric epithets have the binding properties of R-expressions; e.g. see Lasnik and Uriagereka (1988: 39).

We would like to point out that the definition of a pronominal associated with value (e) of the governing-category parameter comes dangerously close to being a definition of an R-expression, which should be free everywhere under principle C of binding theory.

4 But see Hyams (1987) for a revised parametric view, discussed in chapter 7.

5 There is a problem inherent in this conception of the licensing of *pro* subjects. While in adult grammar *pro* subjects are licensed by a Case-assigning category (i.e. Infl), in child grammar it is the latter's absence that serves the same purpose. It is further noted that, on Radford's (1990) view, the lack of Infl only accounts for the licensing of null subjects in early English; the identification of the content of a null subject is considered to occur pragmatically, as in (adult) Chinese. Hyams (1987) also adopts a similar position.

6 Cf. Nishigauchi and Roeper (1987), who independently argue that *pro* is the default empty category that children have access to.

7 It is interesting to note that Radford (1986) also contemplates a similar explanation. He notes that there seem to exist languages (e.g. Norwegian) in which, not unlike the language of native English-speaking children, the clauses might possibly be considered to be headed by the lexical category V rather than by the grammatical category Infl. He further speculates that

> If this is so, then the early type of clausal structure acquired by young English-speaking children may bear important typological similarities to that found in adult grammars of Norwegian-type languages. And this would open up the fascinating possibility that the range of parametric variation found within child grammars mirrors that found within adult grammars. (ibid.: 29)

Surely if there are adult grammars lacking Infl, they do not also lack Case, tense, etc., as child grammars appear to do. This obviously casts severe doubts on the viability of this speculation, indicating that any attempts to relate the typological variation among adult grammars to child grammars are bound to be fraught with many thorny problems.

8 Hyams (1986) notes that, unlike the null-subject parameter, the parameter governing subject inversion does conform to Wexler and Manzini's subset condition, with a language allowing optional subject inversion being a superset of a language that does not permit this type of inversion. So, in this case there is an ordering determined on learnability grounds which, we believe, is quite legitimately convertible into a potential developmental sequence.

6   The distribution and variety of null subjects

1 According to Chomsky (1981), the distinction between nonarguments and quasi-arguments is in part motivated by the fact that in certain cases quasi-arguments can function as controllers of PRO like full referential arguments, as in (1).

(1)a. It sometimes rains after [PRO snowing]
  b. It rained without [PRO snowing] for days and days
  c. It was raining too heavily [PRO to stop in five minutes]
  d. It is too stormy [PRO to last long]

In contrast, nonarguments typically cannot do so. Travis (1984), however, notes that the control facts involved are far from simple. To elaborate, in some *be*-Adj constructions nonargument pleonastics also appear to be able to function as controllers. For example, consider (2a) and (2b), drawn from Travis (1984); (2b) is probably better than (2a). It seems that in these constructions the PRO is more easily controlled by an antecedent in the next higher clause; this conclusion is further supported by (2c).

(2)a. !It was clear that she could do it without PRO being obvious
 b. It was clear without PRO being obvious that she could do it
 c. It was clear that she could do it without PRO being careless

Travis (1984) speculates that the possibility of control might distinguish quasi-argument *and* be-Adj constructions from all other constructions involving nonarguments (see the elaborate hierarchy of constructions involving pleonastic subjects proposed in Travis 1984), rather than just quasi-arguments from nonarguments. We tentatively suggest that *be*-Adj constructions can ambiguously behave like quasi-arguments because they have referential analogues, unlike, say, raising verbs, as is shown respectively in (3i) and (3ii).

(3)i.a. It is certain that John has left Mary
 b. That John has left Mary is certain
 c. It is certain (i.e. some fact is certain)
 ii.a. It seems that John has left Mary
 b. *That John has left Mary seems
 c. *It seems

In fact, it may not be necessary to base the distinction between nonarguments and quasi-arguments on the evidence bearing on control relations. The fact that nonarguments must, and quasi-arguments cannot, be construed with an extraposed NP or clause alone should suffice for the purpose. Also, the following contrasts in English appear to reinforce the assumption that in some sense quasi-arguments are stronger subjects than nonarguments; the latter have to be omitted in some adjunct clauses in English (4a–d), but the former do not appear to be omissible in similar constructions (4e–f).

(4)a. John must have left early, as seems to be the case
 b. !John must have left early, as it seems to be the case
 c. John must have left early, as is obvious
 d. !John must have left early, as it is obvious
 e. *John cannot leave now, as is raining
 f. John cannot leave now, as it is raining

Chomsky (1981) observes further that, in contrast with referential arguments, neither quasi-arguments (5a) nor nonarguments (5b) can be questioned.

(5)a. It rains
 *What rains?
 b. It appears that Mary is gone
 *What appears that Mary is gone?

The reason why the weather-*it* in (5a), and the pure expletive in (6a), cannot be questioned is that both are nonreferential.

2 A word of caution is necessary at this point. It is not certain that the distinctions between the three types of subjects are neatly held across most languages. It is quite possible that a class of predicates that appears in one category in one language appears in another category in a different language. For instance, in some languages the subjects of the atmospheric–temporal predicates are expressed as referential arguments, not as quasi-arguments. Consider the following Hindi–Urdu examples, where the underlined subject is a referential NP.

    a. <u>*Baarish*</u> ho   raahii hai
       rain happen Asp is
       'it is raining'
    b. <u>*Miih*</u> baras rahaa hai
       rain fall Asp is
       'it is raining'

This is, in a way, consistent with the tendency among the subjects of atmospheric–temporal predicates in languages like English to behave as if they are somewhat like referential arguments, in that they appear to be thematic. In the text we shall presume, with the proviso regarding cross-linguistic lexical variation in mind, that the distinctions between referential arguments, quasi-arguments, and nonarguments are in general well motivated.

3 However, McCloskey and Hale remind us that 'Irish is not a language which is in any general sense rich in its system of person–number marking morphology for verbs, though it has sometimes been claimed that this is the criterial difference between languages which show null-subject phenomena and those which do not' (1984: 492).

4 In the spirit of Chomsky (1986b) and Lasnik and Saito (1984), it is possible to assume that a requirement of proper government (i.e. ECP) does not hold of the empty category *pro*; under their approaches the ECP applies only to nonpronominal empty categories, namely the traces of moved elements, and never to pronominal elements *pro* and PRO. At any rate, if it is maintained that long-distance Wh-extraction of subjects is from a postposed position (see section 2.4 above), then the issue loses much of its significance.

    Also note that according to Adams (1987) the direction of government is yet another factor in the licensing, in that a null subject must be governed in the canonical direction.

5 Rizzi (1986a) observes that a limited range of null objects is also possible in Italian; in particular, null objects with arbitrary reference are allowed in this language. Construal with Agr will not be possible in this case, as in Italian there is no agreement between V and its object. Rizzi proposes that the V-licensed *pro* is identified by means of another form of head binding, consisting of coindexation with the appropriate slot in the θ-grid of the verb. The slot is assigned arbitrary interpretation through a special indexing procedure; the assignment of the index *arb* is necessary since a slot in a θ-grid is intrinsically without any features.

6 Many researchers find the PRO theorem to be conceptually and empirically inadequate, following the lead provided by Manzini (1983) and Bouchard (1984). Bouchard (1984: 165ff, 172ff) points out that the logic underlying the so-called PRO theorem is rather dubious. If it is correct that PRO is a pronominal anaphor, then what should follow from binding principles A and B is that PRO does not have a governing category, not that it is ungoverned. Recall that a governing category is defined as a category which contains a pronominal or an anaphor, its governor, and an accessible subject. Now, for PRO not to have a governing category it would not be necessary that it should be both without a governor and without an accessible subject. In fact it should suffice for it not to have an accessible subject (as is generally the case), or not to have a governor.

7 In Saleemi (1988a, 1988b, 1990) the LF part of the Visibility Condition is not considered to be disjunctive, and therefore the licensing schema relies exclusively on Case. More specifically, it is assumed (following Bouchard 1984, and Fabb 1984: 43) that Case can be assigned at any level other than D-structure, including LF, and that phonetically null NPs can meet the visibility requirements in LF by acquiring Case at that level. In keeping with this view of Case assignment it is further postulated there, adopting a proposal by Bouchard (1984), that in null subject languages Case-marking of subjects may be optionally delayed until LF; in common with the present revised account, the previous proposal presupposes that obligatory Case at S-structure requires an NP to be lexically realized at PF, whereas in the event of optionality of syntactic Case an NP need not be so realized, unless some other feature (e.g. focus) forces it to acquire Case in order to be overt.

The present formulation was suggested by an anonymous reviewer; it appears more desirable since the idea of LF Case seems somewhat counterintuitive and redundant, and since this idea might result in overgeneration.

8 Like German, pleonastic pro-drop in Icelandic is also not without exceptions; see Platzack (1987).

9 The distinction between the values (b) and (c) of the parameter would hold to the extent that, all else being equal, languages omit nonarguments and/or quasi-arguments reasonably consistently. Ken Safir (p.c.) has pointed out that a closer examination of a wider range of data might reveal that, once pragmatic interference is set aside, these two values are not actually distinct.

10 Strictly speaking, it is untrue that referential pro-drop is always freely optional. Thus, (a) the distribution of overt pronouns in null-subject languages is generally subject to a focus constraint, so that overt pronouns are typically avoided unless they are required for reasons of emphasis. Further, in certain cases overt pronouns are not possible at all (b) in some or (c) in all null-subject configurations. An example of (b) is Spanish; in this language overt pronouns are excluded if the context demands that they function as bound variables; see this contrast between English and Spanish (examples drawn from Lasnik 1990).

> *Todo el mundo$_i$ piensa que el$_i$ es inteligente
> Everyone$_i$ thinks   he$_i$ is intelligent

The more extreme case (c) is exemplified by Irish. McCloskey and Hale report that Irish is a pro-drop language in a strong sense, in that pro-drop is obligatory in configurations containing synthetic inflected verb forms.

> a. Chuirfinn   (*mé) isteach ar an phost sin
>   put (Condit)   I   in   on that job
>   'I would apply for that job'
> b. Chuirfimis   (*muid) isteach ar an phost sin
>   put (Condit) we   in   on that job
>   'we would apply for that job'

They mention the possibility, however, that the inflected parts of these forms may actually be incorporated pronominals, in which case they could be treated as being in complementary distribution with lexical NPs (1984: 526ff).

11 Baker remarks that 'A language which both allows sentences with no overt NP *and* contains pleonastic pronouns is conceivable, but would be at least doubly-marked and hence rare' (1983: 7). On the optionality of Irish *sé*, Baker further comments: 'It seems impossible to explain this as anything more than lexically marked idiosyncracies of Irish predicates' (ibid.: 41, n 7).

7   Augmented parameter fixation

1 It is noteworthy that, even if the null-subject parameter is binary-valued, our learnability logic will remain basically unaffected so long as the non-null-subject setting is considered to be the unmarked setting, since the languages associated with the marked null-subject setting may nonetheless lack lexical pleonastics.

2 That expletives have homophonous referential or otherwise meaningful analogues is of course not purely accidental; Nishigauchi and Roeper (1987) adduce evidence suggesting that expletives are bootstrapped *via* their meaningful counterparts.

3 Lasnik (1990) is not convinced that the account provided by Mazurkewich and White (1984) really depends on positive-only evidence. He maintains that the solution these authors propose is virtually indistinguishable from one that admits indirect negative evidence, and that in the case under consideration 'there is no obvious way around the need for indirect negative evidence'.

4 Also cf. section 5.1.1, where it was suggested that Wexler and Manzini's formulation of the governing-category parameter is easily relatable to a view of markedness based on gradual change in the opacity of the governing category.

5 A related view is offered in Hyams (to appear), where the inflectional differences between Italian-type and English-type languages are attributed to the parametric distinction that in the former, but not in the latter, the inflections are a feature of the core grammar. The claim is that elements belonging to core grammar emerge earlier than the peripheral features, and that the core option is uniformity of inflection, either manifested in regular paradigms or in the total absence of any inflection. Hence the late acquisition of whatever inflections exist in English-type languages, and the relatively early emergence of an articulated inflectional system in Italian-type languages.

References

Adams, M. 1987. From Old French to the theory of pro-drop. *Natural Language and Linguistic Theory* 5: 1–32

Angluin, D. 1980. Inductive inference of formal languages from positive data. *Information and Control* 45: 117–35

Angluin, D. and Smith, C. H. 1983. Inductive inference: theory and methods. *Computing Surveys* 15: 237–59

Aoun, J. 1985. *A Grammar of Anaphora*. Cambridge, MA: MIT Press

Aoun, J. and Sportiche, D. 1983. On the formal theory of government. *The Linguistic Review* 2: 211–36

Aoun, J., Hornstein, N., Lightfoot, D., and Weinberg, A. 1987. Two types of locality. *Linguistic Inquiry* 18: 537–77

Atkinson, R. M. 1982. *Explanations in the Study of Child Language Development*. Cambridge: Cambridge University Press

1986. Learnability. In P. Fletcher and M. Garman (eds.), *Language Acquisition* (2nd edition). Cambridge: Cambridge University Press

1987. Mechanisms for language acquisition: learning, parameter-setting, and triggering. *First Language* 7: 3–30

Awbery, G. M. 1976. *The Syntax of Welsh: A Transformational Study of the Passive*. Cambridge: Cambridge University Press

Baker, C. L. 1979. Syntactic theory and the projection problem. *Linguistic Inquiry* 10: 533–81

1981. Learnability and the English auxiliary system. In Baker and McCarthy

Baker, C. L. and McCarthy, J. (eds). 1981. *The Logical Problem of Language Acquisition*. Cambridge, MA: MIT Press

Baker, M. 1983. Objects, themes, and lexical rules in Italian. In L. Levin, M. Rappaport and A. Zaenen (eds.), *Papers in Lexical-Functional Grammar*. Bloomington: Indiana University Linguistics Club

1988. *Incorporation: A Theory of Grammatical Function Changing*. Chicago: University of Chicago Press

Bennis, H. and Haegeman, L. 1984. On the status of agreement and relative clauses in West-Flemish. In W. de Geest, and Y. Putseys, (eds.), *Sentential Complementation*. Dordrecht: Foris

Berwick, R. C. 1985. *The Acquisition of Syntactic Knowledge*. Cambridge, MA: MIT Press

1986. Learning from positive-only examples: the subset principle and three case studies. In R. S. Michalski, J. G. Carbonell and T. M. Mitchell (eds.), *Machine Learning: An Artificial Intelligence Approach*, vol. 2. Los Altos, CA: Morgan Kaufmann

Berwick, R. C. and Pilato, S. 1987. Learning syntax by automata induction. *Machine Learning* 2: 9–38

Berwick, R. C. and Weinberg, A. 1984. *The Grammatical Basis of Linguistic Performance: Language Use and Acquisition*. Cambridge, MA: MIT Press

Beukema, F. and Coopmans, P. 1989. A Government-Binding perspective on the imperative in English. *Journal of Linguistics* 25: 417–36

Bloom, P. 1990. Subjectless sentences in child language. *Linguistic Inquiry* 21: 491–504

Borer, H. 1984. *Parametric Syntax: Case Studies in Semitic and Romance Languages*. Dordrecht: Foris

    1989. Anaphoric AGR. In Jaeggli and Safir (eds.)

Borer, H. and Wexler, K. 1987. The maturation of syntax. In Roeper and Williams 1988. The maturation of grammatical principles. Ms., UC-Irvine and MIT

Bouchard, D. 1984. *On the Content of Empty Categories*. Dordrecht: Foris

Bowerman, M. 1987. The 'no negative evidence' problem: how do children avoid constructing an overly general grammar? In J. A. Hawkins (ed.), *Explaining Language Universals*. Oxford: Basil Blackwell

Braine, M. D. S. 1971. On two types of models of the internalization of grammars. In D. Slobin (ed.), *The Ontogenesis of Grammar: A Theoretical Symposium*. New York: Academic Press

Brandi, L. and Cordin, P. 1989. Two Italian dialects and the null subject parameter. In Jaeggli and Safir (eds.)

Bresnan, J. (ed.). 1982. *The Mental Representation of Grammatical Relations*. Cambridge, MA: MIT Press

Brown, R. and Hanlon, C. 1970. Derivational complexity and order of acquisition in child speech. In J. R. Hayes (ed.), *Cognition and the Development of Language*. New York: John Wiley

Buckingham, H. 1989. On triggers. (Comments on Lightfoot 1989)

Catania, A. C. and Harnad, S. 1988. *The Selection of Behaviour – The Operant Behaviorism of B. F. Skinner: Comments and Consequences*. Cambridge: Cambridge University Press

Chao, W. 1980. Pro-drop languages and nonobligatory control. In W. Chao and D. Wheeler (eds.), *University of Massachusetts Occasional Papers in Linguistics* 7: 46–74

Chomsky, N. 1959. A review of B. F. Skinner's *Verbal Behavior, Language* 35: 26–58

    1965. *Aspects of the Theory of Syntax*. Cambridge, MA: MIT Press

    1976. *Reflections on Language*. New York: Pantheon

    1980. *Rules and Representations*. Oxford: Basil Blackwell

    1981. *Lectures on Government and Binding*. Dordrecht: Foris

    1982. *Some Concepts and Consequences of the Theory of Government and Binding*. Cambridge, MA: MIT Press

1986a. *Knowledge of Language: Its Nature, Origin, and Use.* New York: Praeger

1986b. *Barriers.* Cambridge, MA: MIT Press

1987a. On the nature, use and acquisition of language. Kyoto lecture I. Unpublished ms.

1987b. Transformational grammar: past – present – future. Kyoto lecture II. Unpublished ms.

1988. *Language and Problems of Knowledge: The Managua Lectures.* Cambridge, MA: MIT Press

1989. Some notes on economy of derivation and representation. In I. Laka and A. Mahajan (eds.), *Functional Heads and Clause Structure, MIT Working Papers in Linguistics* 10: 43–74

Chomsky, N. and Miller, G. 1963. Introduction to the formal analysis of natural languages. In R. Luce, R. Bush, and E. Galanter (eds.), *Handbook of Mathematical Psychology*, Vol. II. New York: John Wiley

Cinque, G. 1989. Parameter setting in 'instantaneous' and real-time acquisition. (Comments on Lightfoot 1989)

Cohen, D. I. A. 1986. *Introduction to Computer Theory.* New York: John Wiley

Cole, P., Hermon, G. and Sung, L.-M. 1990. Principles and parameters of long-distance reflexives. *Linguistic Inquiry* 21: 1–22

Cook, V. J. 1988. *Chomsky's Universal Grammar: An Introduction.* Oxford: Basil Blackwell

Culicover, P. W. and Wilkins, W. K. 1984. *Locality in Linguistic Theory.* New York: Academic Press

Dell, F. 1981. On the learnability of optional phonological rules. *Linguistic Inquiry* 12: 31–7

Demopoulos, W. and Marras, A. (eds.). 1986. *Language Learning and Concept Acquisition: Foundational Issues.* Norwood, NJ: Ablex

Fabb, N. 1984. Syntactic affixation. Doctoral dissertation, MIT Press

Felix, S. W. 1987. *Cognition and Language Growth.* Dordrecht: Foris

Fodor, J. A. 1975. *The Language of Thought.* Hassocks, Sussex: Harvester Press

1981. The present status of the innateness controversy. In Fodor, J. A., *Representations.* Cambridge, MA: MIT Press

1983. *The Modularity of Mind.* Cambridge, MA: MIT Press

Fukui, N. 1986. A theory of category projection and its applications. Doctoral dissertation, MIT

Gazdar, G., Klein, E., Pullum, G., and Sag, I. 1985. *Generalized Phrase Structure Grammar.* Oxford: Basil Blackwell

Gleitman, L. R. 1981. Maturational determinants of language growth. *Cognition* 10: 103–14

Gold, E. M. 1967. Language identification in the limit. *Information and Control* 10: 447–74

Grimshaw, J. 1979. Complement selection and the lexicon. *Linguistic Inquiry* 10: 279–326

1981. Form, function and the language acquisition device. In Baker and McCarthy

1987. The components of learnability theory. In J. L. Garfield (ed.), *Modularity in Knowledge Representation and Natural-Language Understanding*, Cambridge, MA: MIT Press

Grimshaw, J. and Rosen, S. T. 1990. Knowledge and obedience: the developmental status of the binding theory. *Linguistic Inquiry* 21: 187–222

Grishman, R. 1986. *Computational Linguistics: An Introduction*. Cambridge: Cambridge University Press

Gruber, J. 1967. Topicalization in child language. *Foundations of Language* 3: 37–65

Guilfoyle, E. 1984. The acquisition of tense and the emergence of lexical subjects in child grammars of English. *The McGill Working Papers in Linguistics* 2: 20–30

Hale, K. 1983. Walpiri and the grammar of non-configurational languages. *Natural Language and Linguistic Theory* 1: 5–47

Hasegawa, N. 1985. On the so-called 'zero pronouns' in Japanese. *The Linguistic Review* 4: 289–341

Higginbotham, J. 1984. English is not a context-free language. *Linguistic Inquiry* 15: 225–34

1985. On semantics. *Linguistic Inquiry* 16: 547–93

Hopcroft, J. E. and Ullman, J. D. 1979. *Introduction to Automata Theory, Languages, and Computation*. Reading, MA: Addison-Wesley

Hornstein, N. and Lightfoot, D. 1981a. Introduction. In Hornstein and Lightfoot (eds.)

(eds.) 1981b. *Explanations in Linguistics: The Logical Problem of Language Acquisition*. London: Longman

1987. Predication and PRO. *Language* 63: 23–52

Horrocks, G. 1987. *Generative Grammar*. London: Longman

Huang, C.-T. J. 1982. Logical relations in Chinese and the theory of grammar. Doctoral dissertation, MIT

1984. On the distribution and reference of empty pronouns. *Linguistic Inquiry* 15: 531–74

1987. Remarks on empty categories in Chinese. *Linguistic Inquiry* 18: 321–37

1989. Pro-drop in Chinese: a generalized control theory. In Jaeggli and Safir (eds.)

Hyams, N. 1985. The acquisition of clausal complementation. *Proceedings of WCCFL* 4, Stanford Linguistics Association

1986. *Language Acquisition and the Theory of Parameters*. Dordrecht: Reidel

1987. The setting of the null subject parameter: a reanalysis. Boston University Conference on Child Language Development

1989. The null subject parameter in language acquisition. In Jaeggli and Safir (eds.)

(to appear). The acquisition of inflection: a parameter-setting approach

Hyams, N. and Sigurjónsdóttir, S. (1990). The development of 'long-distance anaphora': a cross-linguistic comparison with special reference to Icelandic. *Language Acquisition* 1: 57–93

Ingram, D. 1989. *First Language Acquisition: Method, Description and Explanation*. Cambridge: Cambridge University Press

Jackendoff, R. S. 1977. *X'-Syntax: A Study of Phrase Structure*. Cambridge, MA: MIT Press

Jaeggli, O. 1982. *Topics in Romance Syntax*. Dordrecht: Foris

Jaeggli, O. and Hyams, N. 1988. Morphological uniformity and the setting of the null subject parameter. *NELS* 18

Jaeggli, O. and Safir, K. 1989a. The null subject parameter and parametric theory. In Jaeggli and Safir (eds.)

1989b. *The Null Subject Parameter*. Dordrecht: Kluwer

Karmiloff-Smith, A. 1987. Some recent issues in the study of language acquisition. In J. Lyons, R. Coates, M. Deuchar and G. Gazdar (eds.), *New Horizons in Linguistics 2*. London: Penguin

Keenan, E. and Comrie, B. 1977. Noun phrase accessibility hierarchy and universal grammar. *Linguistic Inquiry* 8: 63–99

Kempson, R. M. 1988. On the grammar-cognition interface: the principle of full interpretation. In R. M. Kempson (ed.), *Mental Representations: The Interface between Language and Reality*. Cambridge: Cambridge University Press

Kenstowicz, M. 1989. The null subject parameter in modern Arabic dialects. In Jaeggli and Safir (eds.)

Kilby, D. 1987. Typology and universals in Chomsky's theory of grammar. In S. Modgil and C. Modgil (eds.), *Noam Chomsky: Consensus and Controversy*. New York: The Falmer Press

Koopman, H. 1984. *The Syntax of Verbs*. Dordrecht: Foris

Kornai, A. and Pullum, G. 1990. The X-bar theory of phrase structure. *Language* 66: 24–50

Koster, J. 1978. *Locality Principles in Syntax*. Dordrecht: Foris

1984. On binding and control. *Linguistic Inquiry* 15: 417–59

1987. *Domains and Dynasties: The Radical Autonomy of Syntax*. Dordrecht: Foris

Langendoen, D. T. and Postal, P. M. 1984. *The Vastness of Natural Languages*. Oxford: Basil Blackwell

Lasnik, H. 1981. Learnability, restrictiveness, and the evaluation metric. In Baker and McCarthy

1990. On certain substitutes for negative data. In H. Lasnik, *Essays on Restrictiveness and Learnability*. Dordrecht: Reidel

Lasnik, H. and Saito, M. 1984. On the nature of proper government. *Linguistic Inquiry* 15: 235–89

Lasnik, H. and Uriagereka, J. 1988. *A Course in GB Syntax: Lectures on Binding and Empty Categories*. Cambridge, MA: MIT Press

Lebeaux, D. 1987. Comments on Hyams. In Roeper and Williams

Levelt, W. J. M. 1974. *Formal Grammars in Linguistics and Psycholinguistics*, vol. 1: *An Introduction to the Theory of Formal Languages and Automata*; vol. 2: *Applications in Linguistic Theory*; vol. 3: *Psycholinguistic Applications*. The Hague: Mouton

Levy, Y. 1983. It's frogs all the way down. *Cognition* 15: 75–93

Lightfoot, D. 1982. *The Language Lottery: Toward a Biology of Grammars*. Cambridge, MA: MIT Press

1989. The child's trigger experience: degree-0 learnability. (With peer commentary). *Behavioral and Brain Sciences* 12: 321–75

MacWhinney, B. (ed.) 1987. *Mechanisms of Language Acquisition*. Hillsdale, NJ: Lawrence Erlbaum

Manaster-Ramer, A. (ed.) 1987. *Mathematics of Language*. Amsterdam/ Philadelphia: John Benjamins

Manzini, M. R. 1983. On control and control theory. *Linguistic Inquiry* 14: 421–46

1989. Categories and acquisition in the parameters perspective. *UCL Working Papers in Linguistics* 1: 181–91

Manzini, M. R. and Wexler, K. 1987. Parameters, binding theory, and learnability. *Linguistic Inquiry* 18: 413–44

Matthews, R. J. 1979. Are the grammatical sentences of a language a recursive set? *Synthese* 40: 209–24

May, R. 1985. *Logical form: Its Structure and Derivation*. Cambridge, MA: MIT Press

Mazurkewich, I. and White, L. 1984. The acquisition of the dative alternation: unlearning overgeneralizations. *Cognition* 16: 261–83

McCawley, J. D. 1983. Towards plausibility in theories of language acquisition. *Communication and Cognition* 16: 169–83

McCloskey, J. 1986. Inflection and conjunction in modern Irish. *Natural Language and Linguistic Theory* 4: 245–81

McCloskey, J. and Hale, K. 1984. On the syntax of person–number inflection in Modern Irish. *Natural Language and Linguistic Theory* 1: 487–533

McNeill, D. 1966. Developmental psycholinguistics. In F. Smith and G. Miller (eds.), *The Genesis of Language*. Cambridge, MA: MIT Press

Mitchell, T. M. 1978. Version spaces: an approach to concept learning. Doctoral dissertation, Stanford University

1983. Generalization as search. *Artificial Intelligence* 18: 203–26

Montalbetti, M. and Wexler, K. 1985. Binding is linking. *Proceedings of WCCFL* 4: 228–45

Morgan, J. L. 1986. *From Simple Input to Complex Grammar*. Cambridge, MA: MIT Press

Morgan, J. L., Meier, R. P., and Newport, E. L. 1988. Facilitating the acquisition of syntax with transformational cues to phrase structure. Mimeo

Newport, E. L., Gleitman, L. R., and Gleitman, H. 1977. Mother, I'd rather do it myself: some effects and non-effects of maternal speech style. In C. E. Snow and C. A. Ferguson (eds.), *Talking to Children: Language Input and Acquisition*. Cambridge: Cambridge University Press

Nishigauchi, T. and Roeper, T. 1987. Deductive parameters and the growth of empty categories. In Roeper and Williams

Oehrle, R. T. 1985. Implicit negative evidence. Ms., Department of Linguistics, University of Arizona, Tucson

Osherson, D. N., Stob, M., and Weinstein, S. 1984. Learning theory and natural language. *Cognition* 17: 1–28

1986a. *Systems That Learn: An Introduction to Learning Theory for Cognitive and Computer Scientists*. Cambridge, MA: MIT Press

1986b. An analysis of a learning paradigm. In Demopoulos and Marras

Osherson, D. N. and Weinstein, S. 1984a. Formal learning theory. In M. Gazzaniga (ed.), *Handbook of Cognitive Neuroscience*. New York: Plenum

1984b. Models of language acquisition. In P. Marler and H. S. Terrace (eds.), *The Biology of Learning*. Berlin: Springer-Verlag

Partee, B. H. 1978. *Fundamentals of Mathematics for Linguistics*. Dordrecht: Reidel

Pesetsky, D. 1982. Paths and categories. Doctoral dissertation, MIT

Peters, S. 1972. The projection problem: how is a grammar to be selected? In S. Peters (ed.) *Goals of Linguistic Theory*. Englewood Cliffs, NJ: Prentice-Hall

Piattelli-Palmarini, M. (ed.) 1980. *Language and Learning*. London: Routledge and Kegan Paul

1986. The rise of selective theories: a case study and some lessons from immunology. In Demopoulos and Marras

1989. Evolution, selection and cognition: from 'learning' to parameter setting in biology and in the study of language. *Cognition* 31: 1–44

Picallo, M. C. 1984. The Infl node and the null subject parameter. *Linguistic Inquiry* 15: 75–102

Pinker, S. 1979. Formal models of language learning. *Cognition* 7: 217–83

1982. A theory of the acquisition of lexical–functional grammar. In Bresnan

1984. *Language Learnability and Language Development*. Harvard, MA: Harvard University Press

1986. Productivity and conservatism in language acquisition. In Demopoulos and Marras

1987. The bootstrapping problem in language acquisition. In MacWhinney

1989. *Learnability and Cognition: The Acquisition of Argument Structure*. Cambridge, MA: MIT Press

Pinker, S., Lebeaux, D. S., and Frost, L. A. 1987. Productivity and constraints in the acquisition of the passive. *Cognition* 26: 195–267

Platzack, C. 1987. The Scandinavian languages and the null-subject parameter. *Natural Language and Linguistic Theory* 5: 377–401

1990. A grammar without functional categories: a syntactic study of early Swedish child language. Ms., Lund University

Pollock, J.-Y. 1989. Verb movement, Universal Grammar, and the structure of IP. *Linguistic Inquiry* 20: 365–424

Pullum, G. 1983. How many possible human languages are there? *Linguistic Inquiry* 14: 447–67

Radford, A. 1986. Small children's small clauses. *UCNW Research Papers in Linguistics* 1: 1–38

1988a. Small children's small clauses. *Transactions of the Philological Society* 86: 1–46

1988b. *Transformational Syntax: A First Course*. Cambridge: Cambridge University Press

1990. *Syntactic Theory and the Acquisition of English Syntax: The Nature of Early Child Grammars of English*. Oxford: Basil Blackwell

Randall, J. H. 1985. Indirect positive evidence: overturning overgeneralizations in acquisition. Mimeo., Northeastern University

Raposo, E. 1987. Case theory and Infl-to-Comp: the inflected infinitive in European Portuguese. *Linguistic Inquiry* 18: 85–109

Riemsdijk, H. van, and Williams, E. 1986. *Introduction to the Theory of Grammar.* Cambridge, MA: MIT Press

Rizzi, L. 1980. Comments on Chomsky. In J. Mehler (ed.), *Proceedings of the June 1980 Conference on the Cognitive Sciences.* Paris: CNRS. (Cited in Berwick 1985)

1982. *Issues in Italian Syntax.* Dordrecht: Foris

1986a. Null objects in Italian and the theory of *pro. Linguistic Inquiry* 17: 501–57

1986b. On the status of subject clitics in Romance. In O. Jaeggli and C. Silva-Corvalán (eds.), *Studies in Romance Linguistics.* Dordrecht: Foris

Roca, I. M. (ed.) (1990). *Logical Issues in Language Acquisition.* Dordrecht: Foris

Roeper, T. and Williams, E. (eds.) 1987. *Parameter Setting.* Dordrecht: Reidel

Rothstein, S. D. 1983. The syntactic forms of predication. Doctoral dissertation, MIT. Reproduced by IULC, Bloomington (1985)

Safir, K. 1984. Missing subjects in German. In J. Toman (ed.), *Studies in German Grammar.* Dordrecht: Foris

1985. *Syntactic Chains.* Cambridge: CUP

1987. Comments on Wexler and Manzini. In Roeper and Williams

Saleemi, A. P. 1987. The subcategorization of adjectives in English: from principles to application. *Studia Linguistica* 41: 136–53

1988a. Language learnability and empirical plausibility: null subjects and indirect negative evidence. *Papers and Reports in Child Language Development* 27: 89–96. Stanford, CA: Stanford University Press

1988b. Learnability and parameter fixation: The problem of learning in the ontogeny of grammar. Doctoral dissertation, University of Essex

1990. Null subjects, markedness, and parameter fixation. In Roca

Sells, P. 1985. *Lectures on Contemporary Syntactic Theories.* Stanford: CSLI

Shieber, S. M. 1985. Evidence against the context-freeness of natural languages. *Linguistics and Philosophy* 8: 333–43

Shlonsky, U. 1990. *Pro* in Hebrew subject inversion. *Linguistic Inquiry* 21: 263–75

Sigurjónsdóttir, S., Hyams, N. and Chien, Y.-C. 1988. The acquisition of reflexives and pronouns by Icelandic children. *Papers and Reports in Child Language Development* 27: 97–106. Stanford, CA: Stanford University Press

Skinner, B. F. 1957. *Verbal Behavior.* New York: Appleton-Century-Crofts

Slobin, D. I. 1985. Crosslinguistic evidence for the language-making capacity. In D. I. Slobin (ed.), *The Crosslinguistic Study of Language Acquisition*, vol. 2: *Theoretical Issues.* Hillsdale, NJ: Lawrence Erlbaum

Smith, N. V. 1988. Principles, parameters and pragmatics. (Review article on Chomsky 1986a). *Journal of Linguistics* 24: 189–201

1989. Can pragmatics fix parameters? *UCL Working Papers in Linguistics* 1: 169–79 (also in Roca)

Stowell, T. 1981. Origins of phrase structure. Doctoral dissertation, MIT

Taraldsen, K. T. 1978. On the nominative island condition, vacuous application and the *that*-trace filter. Reproduced by IULC, Bloomington (1980)

Travis, L. 1984. Parameters and effects of word order variation. Doctoral dissertation, MIT

Valian, V. 1989. Positive evidence, indirect negative evidence, parameter-setting, and language learning. Ms., Hunter College

1990. Null subjects: a problem for parameter-setting models of language acquisition. *Cognition* 35: 105–22

Wall, R. 1972. *Introduction to Mathematical Linguistics*. Englewood Cliffs, NJ: Prentice-Hall

Wexler, K. 1981. Some issues in the theory of learnability. In Baker and McCarthy

1982. A principle theory for language acquisition. In E. Wanner and L. Gleitman (eds.), *Language Acquisition: The State of the Art*. Cambridge: Cambridge University Press

1987. On the nonconcrete relation between evidence and acquired language. In B. Lust (ed.), *Studies in the Acquisition of Anaphora*, vol. 2: *Applying the Constraints*. Dordrecht: Reidel

1989. Some issues in the growth of Control. Ms., UC-Irvine and MIT

Wexler, K. and Culicover, P. W. 1980. *Formal Principles of Language Acquisition*. Cambridge, MA: MIT Press

Wexler, K. and Manzini, M. R. 1987. Parameters and learnability in binding theory. In Roeper and Williams

White, L. 1981. The responsibility of grammatical theory to acquisition data. In Hornstein and Lightfoot (eds.)

1982. *Grammatical Theory and Language Acquisition*. Dordrecht: Foris

Williams, E. 1980. Predication. *Linguistic Inquiry* 11: 203–38

1981a. Language acquisition, markedness, and phrase structure. In S. Tavakolian (ed.), *Language Acquisition and Linguistic Theory*. Cambridge, MA: MIT Press

1981b. Argument structure and morphology. *The Linguistic Review* 1: 81–114

1987. Introduction. In Roeper and Williams

Xu, L. J. 1986. Free empty category. *Linguistic Inquiry* 17: 75–93

Yang, D. W. 1984. The extended binding theory of anaphors. *Language Research* 19: 169–92

Index

163